Parrot Fire Kris Northern

"Rather than zoom into the fractal you can zoom into the edge of it and continually find the same pattern repeating itself much like the shoreline of a lake viewed from a plane." – **Kris Northern**

Investigations
IN NUMBER, DATA, AND SPACE®

Editorial offices: Glenview, Illinois • Parsippany, New Jersey • New York, New York
Sales offices: Boston, Massachusetts • Duluth, Georgia
Glenview, Illinois • Coppell, Texas • Sacramento, California • Mesa, Arizona

The Investigations curriculum was developed by TERC, Cambridge, MA.

This material is based on work supported by the National Science Foundation ("NSF") under Grant No. ESI-0095450. Any opinions, findings, and conclusions or recommendations expressed in this material are those of the author(s) and do not necessarily reflect the views of the National Science Foundation.

ISBN: 0-328-23764-7

ISBN: 978-0-328-23764-7

6 7 8 9 10-V003-15 14 13 12 11 10 09 08

CC:N2

TERC

Co-Principal Investigators

Susan Jo Russell

Karen Economopoulos

Authors

Lucy Wittenberg
Director Grades 3–5

Karen Economopoulos
Director Grades K–2

Virginia Bastable
(SummerMath for Teachers,
Mt. Holyoke College)

Katie Hickey Bloomfield

Keith Cochran

Darrell Earnest

Arusha Hollister

Nancy Horowitz

Erin Leidl

Megan Murray

Young Oh

Beth W. Perry

Susan Jo Russell

Deborah Schifter
(Education
Development Center)

Kathy Sillman

Note: Unless otherwise noted, all contributors listed above were staff of the Education Research Collaborative at TERC during their work on the curriculum. Other affiliations during the time of development are listed.

Administrative Staff

Amy Taber
Project Manager

Beth Bergeron

Lorraine Brooks

Emi Fujiwara

Contributing Authors

Denise Baumann

Jennifer DiBrienza

Hollee Freeman

Paula Hooper

Jan Mokros

Stephen Monk
(University of Washington)

Mary Beth O'Connor

Judy Storeygard

Cornelia Tierney

Elizabeth Van Cleef

Carol Wright

Technology

Jim Hammerman

Classroom Field Work

Amy Appell

Rachel E. Davis

Traci Higgins

Julia Thompson

Collaborating Teachers

This group of dedicated teachers carried out extensive field testing in their classrooms, met regularly to discuss issues of teaching and learning mathematics, provided feedback to staff, welcomed staff into their classrooms to document students' work, and contributed both suggestions and written material that has been incorporated into the curriculum.

Bethany Altchek

Linda Amaral

Kimberly Beauregard

Barbara Bernard

Nancy Buell

Rose Christiansen

Chris Colbath-Hess

Lisette Colon

Kim Cook

Frances Cooper

Kathleen Drew

Rebeka Eston Salemi

Thomas Fisher

Michael Flynn

Holly Ghazey

Susan Gillis

Danielle Harrington

Elaine Herzog

Francine Hiller

Kirsten Lee Howard

Liliana Klass

Leslie Kramer

Melissa Lee Andrichak

Kelley Lee Sadowski

Jennifer Levitan

Mary Lou LoVecchio

Kristen McEnaney

Maura McGrail

Kathe Millett

Florence Molyneaux

Amy Monkiewicz

Elizabeth Monopoli

Carol Murray

Robyn Musser

Christine Norrman

Deborah O'Brien

Timothy O'Connor

Anne Marie O'Reilly

Mark Paige

Margaret Riddle

Karen Schweitzer

Elisabeth Seyferth

Susan Smith

Debra Sorvillo

Shoshanah Starr

Janice Szymaszek

Karen Tobin

JoAnn Trauschke

Ana Vaisenstein

Yvonne Watson

Michelle Woods

Mary Wright

Advisors

Deborah Lowenberg Ball,
University of Michigan

Hyman Bass, Professor of Mathematics and Mathematics Education
University of Michigan

Mary Canner, Principal, Natick Public Schools

Thomas Carpenter, Professor of Curriculum and Instruction,
University of Wisconsin-Madison

Janis Freckmann, Elementary Mathematics Coordinator,
Milwaukee Public Schools

Lynne Godfrey, Mathematics Coach,
Cambridge Public Schools

Ginger Hanlon, Instructional Specialist in Mathematics,
New York City Public Schools

DeAnn Huinker, Director, Center for Mathematics and
Science Education Research, University of Wisconsin-Milwaukee

James Kaput, Professor of Mathematics, University of
Massachusetts-Dartmouth

Kate Kline, Associate Professor, Department of Mathematics
and Statistics, Western Michigan University

Jim Lewis, Professor of Mathematics,
University of Nebraska-Lincoln

William McCallum, Professor of Mathematics,
University of Arizona

Harriet Pollatsek, Professor of Mathematics,
Mount Holyoke College

Debra Shein-Gerson, Elementary Mathematics Specialist,
Weston Public Schools

Gary Shevell, Assistant Principal,
New York City Public Schools

Liz Sweeney, Elementary Math Department,
Boston Public Schools

Lucy West, Consultant, Metamorphosis:
Teaching Learning Communities, Inc.

This revision of the curriculum was built on the work of the many
authors who contributed to the first edition (published between
1994 and 1998). We acknowledge the critical contributions of
these authors in developing the content and pedagogy of
Investigations:

Authors

Joan Akers

Michael T. Battista

Douglas H. Clements

Karen Economopoulos

Marlene Kliman

Jan Mokros

Megan Murray

Ricardo Nemirovsky

Andee Rubin

Susan Jo Russell

Cornelia Tierney

Contributing Authors

Mary Berle-Carman

Rebecca B. Corwin

Rebeka Eston

Claryce Evans

Anne Goodrow

Cliff Konold

Chris Mainhart

Sue McMillen

Jerrie Moffet

Tracy Noble

Kim O'Neil

Mark Ogonowski

Julie Sarama

Amy Shulman Weinberg

Margie Singer

Virginia Woolley

Tracey Wright

Contents

UNIT 3

Thousands of Miles, Thousands of Seats

Investigations

CURRICULUM

Overview of Program Components

FOR TEACHERS

The **Curriculum Units** are the teaching guides. (See far right.)

Implementing Investigations in Grade 5 offers suggestions for implementing the curriculum. It also contains a comprehensive index.

The **Resources Binder** contains all the Resource Masters and Transparencies that support instruction. (Also available on CD.) The binder also includes a student software CD.

FOR STUDENTS

The **Student Activity Book** contains the consumable student pages (Recording Sheets, Homework, Practice, and so on).

The **Student Math Handbook** contains Math Words and Ideas pages and Games directions.

The *Investigations* Curriculum

Investigations in Number, Data, and Space® is a K–5 mathematics curriculum designed to engage students in making sense of mathematical ideas. Six major goals guided the development of the *Investigations in Number, Data, and Space*® curriculum. The curriculum is designed to:

- Support students to make sense of mathematics and learn that they can be mathematical thinkers

- Focus on computational fluency with whole numbers as a major goal of the elementary grades

- Provide substantive work in important areas of mathematics—rational numbers, geometry, measurement, data, and early algebra—and connections among them

- Emphasize reasoning about mathematical ideas

- Communicate mathematics content and pedagogy to teachers

- Engage the range of learners in understanding mathematics

Underlying these goals are three guiding principles that are touchstones for the *Investigations* team as we approach both students and teachers as agents of their own learning:

1. *Students have mathematical ideas.* Students come to school with ideas about numbers, shapes, measurements, patterns, and data. If given the opportunity to learn in an environment that stresses making sense of mathematics, students build on the ideas they already have and learn about new mathematics they have never encountered. Students learn that they are capable of having mathematical ideas, applying what they know to new situations, and thinking and reasoning about unfamiliar problems.

2. *Teachers are engaged in ongoing learning* about mathematics content, pedagogy, and student learning. The curriculum provides material for professional development, to be used by teachers individually or in groups, that supports teachers' continued learning as they use the curriculum over several years. The *Investigations* curriculum materials are designed as much to be a dialogue with teachers as to be a core of content for students.

3. *Teachers collaborate with the students and curriculum materials* to create the curriculum as enacted in the classroom. The only way for a good curriculum to be used well is for teachers to be active participants in implementing it. Teachers use the curriculum to maintain a clear, focused, and coherent agenda for mathematics teaching. At the same time, they observe and listen carefully to students, try to understand how they are thinking, and make teaching decisions based on these observations.

Investigations is based on experience from research and practice, including field testing that involved documentation of thousands of hours in classrooms, observations of students, input from teachers, and analysis of student work. As a result, the curriculum addresses the learning needs of real students in a wide range of classrooms and communities. The investigations are carefully designed to invite all students into mathematics—girls and boys; members of diverse cultural, ethnic, and language groups; and students with a wide variety of strengths, needs, and interests.

Based on this extensive classroom testing, the curriculum takes seriously the time students need to develop a strong conceptual foundation and skills based on that foundation. Each curriculum unit focuses on an area of content in depth, providing time for students to develop and practice ideas across a variety of activities and contexts that build on each other. Daily guidelines for time spent on class sessions, Classroom Routines (K–3), and Ten-Minute Math (3–5) reflect the commitment to devoting adequate time to mathematics in each school day.

About This Curriculum Unit

This **Curriculum Unit** is one of nine teaching guides in Grade 5. The third unit in Grade 5 is *Thousands of Miles, Thousands of Seats.*

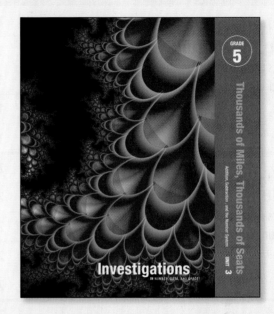

- The **Introduction and Overview** section organizes and presents the instructional materials, provides background information, and highlights important features specific to this unit.

- Each Curriculum Unit contains several **Investigations.** Each Investigation focuses on a set of related mathematical ideas.

- Investigations are divided into one-hour **Sessions,** or lessons.

- Sessions have a combination of these parts: **Activity, Discussion, Math Workshop, Assessment Activity,** and **Session Follow-Up.**

- Each session also has one or more **Ten-Minute Math** activities that are done outside of math time.

- At the back of the book is a collection of **Teacher Notes** and **Dialogue Boxes** that provide professional development related to the unit.

- Also included at the back of the book are the **Student Math Handbook** pages for this unit.

- The **Index** provides a way to look up important words or terms.

Overview

O F   T H I S   U N I T

Investigation	Session	Day	
INVESTIGATION 1 **Using Place Values** Students use place-value relationships and multiples of 10, 100, and 1,000 to add and subtract large numbers.	**1.1** Working with the 10,000 Chart	1	
	1.2 Assessment: Numbers on the 10,000 Chart	2	
	1.3 How Many Steps to 10,000?	3	
	1.4 Adding and Subtracting Large Numbers	4	
	1.5 Adding and Subtracting Large Numbers, *continued*	5	
INVESTIGATION 2 **Studying Subtraction** Students practice and investigate various strategies for subtracting large numbers, including the U.S. algorithm.	**2.1** Naming Subtraction Strategies	6	
	2.2 Practicing Subtraction	7	
	2.3 Subtraction Starter Problems	8	
	2.4 Studying the U.S. Algorithm	9	
	2.5 Assessment: Subtraction Problems	10	
INVESTIGATION 3 **Adding and Subtracting Large Numbers** Students refine various strategies and use what they know about place value to solve addition and subtraction problems involving large numbers.	**3.1** Assessment: Division Facts and *Close to 7,500*	11	
	3.2 Stadium Data	12	
	3.3 Assessment: Numbers to 100,000 and Rock On!	13	
	3.4 Rock On!, *continued*	14	
	3.5 End-of-Unit Assessment	15	

Each *Investigations* session has some combination of these five parts: **Activity, Discussion, Math Workshop, Assessment Activity,** and **Session Follow-Up.** These session parts are indicated in the chart below. Each session also has one or more **Ten-Minute Math** activities that are done outside of math time.

Ten-Minute Math

Activity	Discussion	Math Workshop	Assessment Activity	Session Follow-Up	Practicing Place Value	Estimation and Number Sense: Closest Estimate
●●●				●	●	
●●			●	●	●	
●●●				●	●	
●●		●		●	●	
	●	●		●		●
●●	●			●		●
●	●			●		●
●●	●			●		●
●		●		●	●	
	●	●	●	●	●	
●	●		●	●	●	
●	●			●	●	
	●	●		●		●
	●	●		●		●
	●		●	●	●	

Mathematics

Thousands of Miles, Thousands of Seats is the second Grade 5 unit in the number and operations strand of *Investigations*. These units develop ideas about the meaning of operations with whole numbers, the development of computational fluency, the structure of place value and the base-ten number system, and generalizations about numbers and operations.

LOOKING BACK The work in this unit assumes that students bring to Grade 5 a great deal of knowledge about place value and the operations of addition and subtraction. This unit assumes that students know their addition combinations and related subtraction problems, are fluent with addition strategies for solving multidigit problems, and have at least one strategy they can use to solve multidigit subtraction problems.

Students have studied properties of the operations of addition and subtraction and should know a great deal about how these operations work. For example, students should know that addition is commutative (that is, the order of two addends in an addition expression can be changed without affecting the sum) and subtraction is not. They should be very familiar with the types of situations in which addition and subtraction are used and should be able to apply these operations to a variety of problems, including joining two quantities, removing one quantity from a larger quantity, comparing two quantities, and finding a missing part. Fourth-grade students worked extensively with 1,000, and they investigated multiples of 1,000 up to 10,000. They should understand how 10,000 is composed of ten 1,000s or of one hundred 100s, and they should be able to interpret the place value of digits in large numbers.

If some of your students do not have this background, consider working with a small group or asking a support person to work with a small group, using the Grade 4 unit *Landmarks and Large Numbers*.

This unit focuses on 3 Mathematical Emphases:

1 The Base-Ten Number System Extending knowledge of the number system to 100,000 and beyond

Math Focus Points

◆ Reading, writing, and sequencing numbers to 10,000 and 100,000

◆ Understanding the place-value relationships between 10, 100, 1,000, and 10,000

◆ Learning the names of places larger than 100,000: million, billion, trillion

In order for students to work comfortably and fluently with large numbers, it is important that they develop a solid understanding of how the number system extends to large numbers. This unit provides students with experience that focuses on numbers to the hundred thousands and also provides exposure to larger numbers. In Investigation 1, students use a 10,000 chart to read, write, and sequence numbers to 10,000. In order to emphasize the relationship of 10,000 to 1,000 and to 100, this chart is arranged into 100 rows with 100 squares in each row. Each group of 10 rows is marked by a heavier line so that the ten 10-by-100 rectangles, each of which contains 1,000 squares, stand out. Students use this chart to practice writing and sequencing numbers and for considering relationships between large numbers such as these: How much larger is 9,435 than 8,435? Than 9,335? Than 9,005?

In this unit, students work on decomposing numbers in a variety of ways in order to understand how the way we write and say numbers relates to the quantities they represent. This work goes beyond simply being able to say that 9,765 is composed of "9 thousands, 7 hundreds, 6 tens, and 5 ones." In fact, students may learn to say this without truly understanding the relationships between thousands and hundreds, hundreds and tens, and tens and ones.

Decomposing numbers flexibly supports students' continued work on understanding the place value of numbers in our base-ten number system and developing computational fluency.

9,765 = 9 thousands + 7 hundreds + 6 tens + 5 ones

_____ hundreds + 65 ones

_____ thousands + 17 hundreds + 65

_____ thousands + 57 hundreds + 65

As the unit continues, students focus on numbers up to 100,000. They also write and name even larger numbers: millions, billions, trillions.

2 Computational Fluency Adding and subtracting accurately and efficiently

Math Focus Points

◆ Adding and subtracting multiples of 100 and 1,000

◆ Finding the difference between a number and 10,000

◆ Finding combinations of 3-digit numbers that add to 1,000

◆ Solving addition and subtraction problems with large numbers by focusing on the place value of the digits

◆ Solving whole-number addition and subtraction problems efficiently

◆ Using clear and concise notation for recording addition and subtraction strategies

◆ Interpreting and solving multistep problems

The activities with the 10,000 chart include adding and subtracting multiples of 100 and 1,000. The arrangement of the chart in rows of 100 helps students visualize the effect of adding or subtracting these multiples. This work lays the foundation for many of the addition and subtraction strategies that students use and for estimating reasonable answers to multidigit addition and subtraction problems.

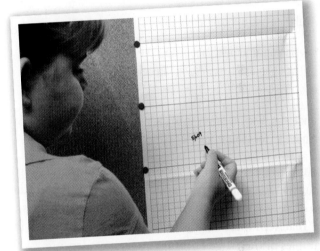

Students use the 10,000 chart to compare the digits in a number such as 5,609 to the sums in problems such as 5,609 + 3,000 or 5,609 + 700.

Building on students' work in Grade 4, this unit provides more practice with adding larger numbers. It also gives students opportunities to apply their understanding of addition in multistep problems with large numbers. Students develop increased fluency in subtraction as they study a range of subtraction strategies, learn how to apply their strategies to larger numbers, and think through how to apply subtraction in new situations. As students work with both addition and subtraction, they learn that they can generalize the strategies they understand to solve problems with very large numbers.

3 Whole-Number Operations **Examining and using strategies for subtracting whole numbers**

Math Focus Points

◆ Identifying, describing, and comparing subtraction strategies by focusing on how each strategy starts

◆ Analyzing and using different subtraction strategies

◆ Developing arguments about how the differences represented by two subtraction expressions are related (e.g., 1,208 − 297 and 1,208 − 300)

◆ Understanding the meaning of the steps and notation of the U.S. algorithm for subtraction

In this unit, as students consolidate their understanding of subtraction and practice and refine their strategies, they also classify and analyze the logic of different strategies. See **Teacher Note:** Subtraction Strategies on page 119 for examples of the range of strategies fifth graders use.

The purpose of this work is for students to increase their flexibility in choosing subtraction strategies as well as to increase their knowledge of the properties of subtraction by thinking through how new strategies work. For example, in the discussion "Do I Add or Subtract?" in Session 2.3, students consider the relationship between the following two subtraction expressions:

$$1,208 - 297 \qquad 1,208 - 300$$

How can the easier problem, 1,208 − 300, be used to solve the more difficult one? This and other subtraction problems lend themselves to changing one of the numbers and then adjusting the difference. However, even if students do not eventually adopt this strategy, by studying it they learn more about how subtraction works, and they strengthen their understanding of generalizations about the

operations that connect arithmetic to algebra. See "Algebra Connections in This Unit," page 16, and **Teacher Note:** Reasoning and Proof in Mathematics, page 125. Similarly, through a study of the steps and notation of the U.S. algorithm, students think through how regrouping the first number in a subtraction problem enables subtracting by place with only positive numbers in the results. See **Teacher Note:** Why Study the U.S. Conventional Algorithms? on page 128.

This Unit also focuses on

◆ Using story contexts and representations, such as number lines, to explain and justify solutions to subtraction problems

◆ Solving division problems related to the multiplication combinations to 12 × 12 (the division facts, e.g., 64 ÷ 8, 54 ÷ 6) with fluency

A Note About Calculators In life, those of us who routinely compute with numbers of the size students encounter in this unit frequently use calculators. Generally, calculators should be available in the classroom, and students should be competent in solving problems with calculators as a life tool. In this unit, students should continue to develop the habit of estimating what a reasonable answer should be to any problem before they calculate. This skill is essential to multidigit calculation, whether done mentally, on paper, or with a calculator. It is also important for students to have the confidence and competence to solve problems mentally as well as by using paper-and-pencil calculations. Therefore, in this unit, students solve problems without the calculator in order to understand how the logic of the computation strategies they use with smaller numbers generalizes to larger numbers. Thinking through the logic of unfamiliar strategies in order to learn more about the operation of subtraction requires that they carry out all the steps themselves; these steps would be unavailable for them to consider if they used a calculator.

This unit finalizes students' work with addition and subtraction of whole numbers in the *Investigations* curriculum. They continue to use knowledge of place value, addition, and subtraction as they complete the rest of this curriculum, particularly in *How Many People? How Many Teams?*, which continues work with multiplication and division. They will revisit addition and subtraction beyond Grade 5 as they work with integers, rational numbers, and variables.

Ten-Minute Math activities focus on

◆ Recognizing and interpreting the value of each digit in 4- and 5-digit numbers

◆ Finding different combinations of a number, using only 1,000s, 100s, 10s, and 1s and recognizing their equivalency (i.e., 1 hundred, 3 tens, and 7 ones = 12 tens and 17 ones, etc.)

◆ Reading and writing numbers up to 100,000

◆ Adding multiples of 10 to, and subtracting multiples of 10 from, 4- and 5-digit numbers

◆ Estimating solutions to 2- and 3-digit multiplication and division problems

◆ Breaking apart, reordering, or changing numbers mentally to determine a reasonable estimate

Technology Note

Getting Started with the *LogoPaths* Software Students are formally introduced to the *LogoPaths* software in the 2-D Geometry and Measurement unit *Measuring Polygons,* the fifth unit in the Grade 5 sequence. However, if you plan to use the software this year, we recommend that students have access to the software **outside of math time** starting with this unit in order to return to *Feed the Turtle,* a *LogoPaths* activity from Grade 3, and to spend time with the *Free Explore* option. For information about the *LogoPaths* software and directions for *Feed the Turtle,* refer to the *Software Support Reference Guide* found on the CD. See **Part 5: Technology in *Investigations*** in *Implementing Investigations in Grade 5:* Introducing and Managing the *LogoPaths* Software in Grade 5.

Assessment

IN THIS UNIT

ONGOING ASSESSMENT: Observing Students at Work

The following sessions provide **Ongoing Assessment: Observing Students at Work** opportunities:

- **Session 1.1, pp. 28 and 31**
- **Session 1.2, p. 35**
- **Session 1.3, pp. 38 and 41**
- **Session 1.4, p. 49**

- **Session 2.1, pp. 60 and 62**
- **Session 2.2, p. 67**
- **Session 2.3, p. 72**
- **Session 2.4, p. 78**

- **Session 3.1, pp. 89 and 92**
- **Session 3.2, p. 95**
- **Session 3.3, p. 101**
- **Session 3.5, p. 111**

WRITING OPPORTUNITIES

The following sessions have **writing** opportunities for students to explain their mathematical thinking:

- **Session 1.1, p. 31**
  Student Activity Book, p. 1

- **Session 1.5, p. 54**
  Student Activity Book, p. 19

- **Session 2.2, p. 67**
  Student Activity Book, p. 28

- **Session 3.3, p. 103**
  Student Activity Book, p. 63

PORTFOLIO OPPORTUNITIES

The following sessions have work appropriate for a **portfolio:**

- **Session 1.4, p. 48**
  Student Activity Book, pp. 13–14

- **Session 2.3, pp. 70 and 71**
  Student Activity Book, pp. 31–32

- **Session 2.4 p. 80**
  Student Activity Book, pp. 39–40

- **Session 2.5, p. 83**
  M15, Assessment: Subtraction Problems

- **Session 3.1, p. 91**
  M18, Assessment: Division Facts

- **Sessions 3.3 and 3.4, pp. 100, 101, 103, and 108**
  Student Activity Book, pp. 59–63

- **Session 3.5, p. 111**
  M20, End-of-Unit Assessment

Assessing the Benchmarks

Observing students as they engage in conversation about their ideas is a primary means to assess their mathematical understanding. Consider all of your students' work, not just the written assessments. See the chart below for suggestions about key activities to observe.

 Checklist Available

Benchmarks in This Unit	Key Activities to Observe	Assessment
1. Read, write, and sequence numbers up to 100,000.	**Session 1.2:** Numbers on the 10,000 Chart **Ten-Minute Math:** Practicing Place Value	**Sessions 1.2, 3.3, 3.4:** Reading, Writing, and Sequencing Numbers to 100,000 ✓
2. Solve subtraction problems accurately and efficiently, choosing from a variety of strategies.	**Session 2.1:** Practicing Subtraction **Session 2.3:** Starter Problems	**Session 2.5 Assessment Activity:** Subtraction Problems **Session 3.5 End-of-Unit Assessment:** Problems 1 and 2
3. Demonstrate fluency with division problems related to the multiplication combinations to 12 × 12 (division facts).		**Session 3.1: Assessment Activity:** Division Facts

Relating the Mathematical Emphases to the Benchmarks

Mathematical Emphases	Benchmarks
The Base-Ten Number System Extending knowledge of the number system to 100,000 and beyond	1
Computational Fluency Adding and subtracting accurately and efficiently	2
Whole-Number Operations Examining and using strategies for subtracting whole numbers	2

Algebra Connections

IN THIS UNIT

In this unit, your students will have opportunities to engage with ideas that lay a foundation for algebra. Ten- and eleven-year-olds can and do think algebraically. Part of the work of Grade 5 is helping students learn to verbalize and represent those thoughts both as a way to engage with generalizations about numbers and operations and as a foundation for meaningful use of algebraic notation in the future. **Note:** Although algebraic notation is not introduced in this unit, students will work with notation in *Growth Patterns*.

Exploring the Inverse Relationship Between Addition and Subtraction

Consider this vignette in which a fifth-grade class is discussing strategies for finding how far it is from 854 to 10,000.

Janet: I started with 854 and added up until I got to 10,000. The answer is 9,146.

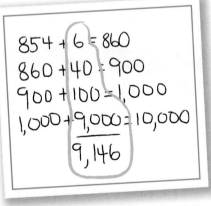

$$854 + 6 = 860$$
$$860 + 40 = 900$$
$$900 + 100 = 1,000$$
$$1,000 + 9,000 = 10,000$$
$$9,146$$

Janet's Work

Terrence: I pictured sort of a number line, but also the 10,000 chart in my mind. I started at 10,000 and knew I had to go a long way back to get to 854. First I went back 9,000 and landed at 1,000. Then I went back 100 and landed on 900 and then I knew I had to go back 40 more to get to 860. It was just 6 more back after that. My answer was 9,146 too, but I subtracted. Here's what I wrote.

$$10,000 - 9,000 = 1,000$$
$$1,000 - 100 = 900$$
$$900 - 40 = 860$$
$$860 - 6 = 854$$

Terrence's Work

Teacher: Janet used a strategy that involved adding up and Terrence used one that involved subtracting. They were solving the same problem. How can that be?

In this vignette, students use different approaches to solve a problem adults might represent as $10,000 - 854 = ?$ Janet thinks of the problem as $854 + ? = 10,000$; Terrence's work is based on $10,000 - ? = 854$. Underlying these approaches is a relationship between addition and subtraction expressed as symbols: if $a + b = c$ then $c - b = a$ and $c - a = b$. In this unit, students will call upon this property to solve subtraction problems which involve comparison or missing addends, to determine how far a given number is from 10,000 and in playing games such as *Close to 7,500*.

Let us return to the vignette to see how the class responded to the teacher's challenge to explain how the same problem could be solved with addition or subtraction.

Lourdes: I am thinking of it as distance. Like, if I have to travel 10,000 miles and I have already traveled 854 miles. I have 9,146 miles still to go. I can write $854 + 9,146 = 10,000$ or $10,000 - 854 = 9,146$. It is just different ways to say that 854 and 9,146 make up 10,000.

Charles: I have this picture in my mind. There is this kind of circle with 10,000 in it. You break the circle apart with a line; one part has some amount and the other part has the rest. You can write different equations to say the two parts make up the 10,000. If you start with the 10,000, you subtract. If you start with the parts, you add. It is saying the same thing.

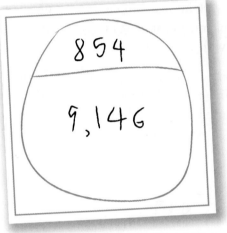

Charles's Work

In this vignette, Lourdes creates a story context to express the relationship between addition and subtraction. Charles uses a mental image which he can interpret as representing either addition or subtraction. Other students might have called upon a number line model or referred to the 10,000 chart. When such representations are shared, students should be encouraged to explain the connections among the diagram, the story context, and the arithmetic expressions to help them articulate their reasoning. What addition statement matches the diagram? How does this subtraction statement match the diagram? What in the story problem matches with this subtraction sentence? What arithmetic expression matches this part of the diagram? Even though students are building images based on specific examples, they are forming connections between these images and the operations of addition and subtraction.

Examining Equivalent Problems In Addition and Subtraction

In this unit, students will solve addition and subtraction problems by transforming them into new problems that have the same answers as the original problems.

Nora: I solved $396 + 475$ by changing the first number to 400. Since I added 4 to 396, I have to subtract 4 from 475. So, I add $400 + 471$ and have the total as 871.

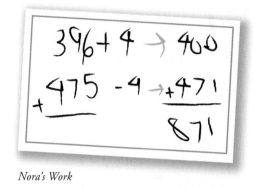

Nora's Work

Renaldo: I had a different problem, and I did it that way, too. Only I added and subtracted a different number. To do $478 + 325$, I changed the first number to 480 and the second number to 323. I got 803.

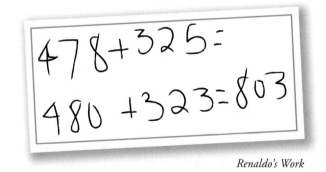

Renaldo's Work

Teacher: Do you think this will always work? Can you explain what is happening with stories, diagrams, or number lines?

This vignette illustrates an important computational strategy students will use in this unit. It also shows how the teacher's questions lead to an examination of the mathematical principles that underlie such a strategy. For more information on students' arguments about equivalent problems in addition, see **Teacher Note:** Reasoning and Proof in Mathematics on page 125.

Nora: I also tried the same thing with a subtraction problem, but it doesn't work.

Teacher: What did you do?

Nora: I was solving $97 - 39$. I wanted the 39 to be a 40. Since I added a 1, I figured I needed to subtract a 1 from 97. That made it $96 - 40 = 56$. But that isn't right. When I did it by adding up, I got 58.

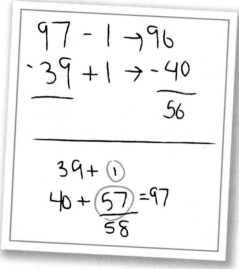

Nora's Work

Teacher: This is an interesting question Nora has brought to our attention. In addition, we know that $97 + 39 = 96 + 40$. Nora tried to do something like that for subtraction and got the wrong answer. Is there a way to change $97 - 39$ to make it easier? Can you be sure your method is correct?

Students often try to use strategies that worked for addition, with a subtraction problem. As they explore how to modify the strategies, but they are not only developing good computation methods, but they are also exploring the differences between the operations of addition and subtraction.

Let us return to the vignette to see how the class responded. Students work in small groups drawing diagrams, creating story problems, and sharing ideas about how to compare $97 - 39$ with $97 - 40$.

Margaret: I was thinking about spending money. If I buy something that is $39 and I subtract $40 to make it easy, I subtracted too much. I would have to add 1 to the answer to get the final answer. The answer to $97 - 39$ should be 1 more than the answer to $97 - 40$.

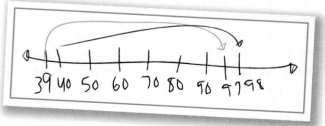

Margaret's Work

Stuart: I thought about the number line and how far apart 97 and 39 are. If you change the 39 to a 40, you have moved over to the right one step and so you have to do that same thing to the 97: change it to 98. So then it must be that $97 - 39 = 98 - 40$.

Stuart's Work

In this vignette, Margaret used a story context and Stuart used a number line to model the subtraction problem. Other students may have built a model with cubes or drawn a diagram to model the subtraction. Such representations of subtraction support students as they think through the steps of various computational strategies. They also support students in articulating generalizations about the operation of subtraction. For instance, in later years Stuart's strategy will be expressed in more formal terms as $(a - b) = (a + 1) - (b + 1)$.

Investigations students are encouraged to verbalize the generalizations they see about numbers and operations, and to explain and justify them using materials and tools, such as cubes or diagrams. For most adults, notation such as the use of variables, operations, and equal signs is the chief identifying feature of algebra. The notation, however, expresses rules about how operations work, which students can reason out for themselves. This reasoning—about how numbers can be put together and taken apart under different operations—not the notation, is the work of elementary students in algebra.

Note: In the text for the sessions, you will find Algebra Notes that identify where these early algebra discussions are likely to arise. Some of the **Teacher Notes** and **Dialogue Boxes** further elaborate the ideas and illustrate students' conversations about them.

Ten-Minute Math

IN THIS UNIT

Ten-Minute Math offers practice and review of key concepts for this grade level. These daily activities, to be done in ten minutes outside of math class, are introduced in a unit and repeated throughout the grade. Specific directions for the day's activity are provided in each session. For the full description and variations of each classroom activity, see *Implementing Investigations in Grade 5*.

Activity	Introduced	Full Description of Activity and Its Variations
Practicing Place Value	Unit 3, Session 1.1 (this unit)	*Implementing Investigations in Grade 5*
Estimation and Number Sense: Closest Estimate	Unit 3, Session 1.4 (this unit)	*Implementing Investigations in Grade 5*

Practicing Place Value

Students practice reading, writing, and saying numbers up to 100,000. They add and subtract multiples of 10 and examine how these operations increase or decrease the values of the digits in each place. Students develop flexibility in decomposing numbers as they break numbers into thousands, hundreds, tens, and ones in various ways and demonstrate their equivalence.

Math Focus Points

◆ Recognizing and interpreting the value of each digit in 4- and 5-digit numbers

◆ Finding different combinations of a number, using only 1,000s, 100s, 10s, and 1s and recognizing their equivalency (i.e. 1 hundred, 3 tens, and 7 ones = 12 tens and 17 ones, etc.)

◆ Reading and writing numbers up to 100,000

◆ Adding multiples of 10 to, and subtracting multiples of 10 from, 4- and 5-digit numbers

Estimation and Number Sense: Closest Estimate

Students choose the closest estimate of a given multiplication or division problem by computing mentally. They discuss their strategies for finding the estimate, including changing numbers to a landmark and breaking numbers apart for easier computation.

Math Focus Points

◆ Estimating solutions to 2- and 3-digit multiplication and division problems

◆ Breaking apart, reordering, or changing numbers mentally to determine a reasonable estimate

Practice and Review

IN THIS UNIT

Practice and review play a critical role in the *Investigations* program. The following components and features are available to provide regular reinforcement of key mathematical concepts and procedures.

Books	Features	In This Unit ...
Curriculum Unit	**Ten-Minute Math** offers practice and review of key concepts for this grade level. These daily activities, to be done in ten minutes outside of math class, are introduced in a unit and repeated throughout the grade. Specific directions for the day's activity are provided in each session. For the full description and variations of each classroom activity, see *Implementing Investigations in Grade 5*.	• **All sessions**
Student Activity Book	**Daily Practice** pages in the *Student Activity Book* provide one of three types of written practice: **reinforcement** of the content of the unit, **ongoing review,** or **enrichment** opportunities. Some Daily Practice pages will also have Ongoing Review items with multiple-choice problems similar to those on standardized tests.	• **All sessions**
	Homework pages in the *Student Activity Book* are an extension of the work done in class. At times they help students prepare for upcoming activities.	• **Session 1.2** • **Session 2.5** • **Session 1.3** • **Session 3.1** • **Session 1.4** • **Session 3.2** • **Session 2.1** • **Session 3.3** • **Session 2.2** • **Session 3.4** • **Session 2.4**
Student Math Handbook	**Math Words and Ideas** in the *Student Math Handbook* are pages that summarize key words and ideas. Most Words and Ideas pages have at least one exercise.	• **Student Math Handbook, pp. 6–13**
	Games pages are found in a section of the *Student Math Handbook*.	• **Student Math Handbook, pp. G2, G3**

Supporting the Range of Learners

Sessions	1.1	1.2	1.3	1.4	2.1	2.2	2.3	2.4	3.1	3.2	3.3	3.5
Intervention			•	•	•	•	•	•	•	•	•	•
Extension			•		•	•		•		•	•	
ELL	•	•								•		

Intervention

Suggestions are made to support and engage students who are having difficulty with a particular idea, activity, or problem.

Extension

Suggestions are made to support and engage students who finish early or who may be ready for additional challenge.

English Language Learners (ELL)

Since students in this unit work with numbers to 100,000 and beyond, they need a good understanding of place value. English Language Learners will benefit from reviewing place names to 10,000 and the names of numbers in the hundreds and thousands. The Math Words and Ideas pages on place value in the *Student Math Handbook* can be a particularly useful reference for the English Language Learners in your classroom.

A number of activities require students to make estimates. English Language Learners may need help understanding the difference between estimating and finding an *exact* value. "*About* how many students in our class have brown hair? Let's *estimate* a number." If students are not sure what you are asking, make an estimate and write it down. "I *estimate* that about 10 students have brown hair. Am I right? Let's count to see *exactly* how many students have brown hair." Count aloud to get a precise figure and write that

down beside the estimate. "How did we get an *estimate?* How did we get an *exact* number?" Be sure to stress that an estimate is an educated guess and should be a reasonable amount.

In order to make comparisons between large numbers, English Language Learners need to know how to use comparative and superlative terms in English. You can provide a simple demonstration, using pictures or objects, to illustrate these language structures.

Students will need to use sequence-related terminology as they identify steps for solving problems. Discuss and list words such as *first, next, then,* and *after* on a chart or card. Students can refer to these words when explaining their strategies during class discussions.

Working with the Range of Learners: Classroom Cases is a set of episodes written by teachers that focuses on meeting the needs of the range of learners in the classroom. In the first section, *Setting up the Mathematical Community,* teachers write about how they create a supportive and productive learning environment in their classrooms. In the next section, *Accommodations for Learning,* teachers focus on specific modifications they make to meet the needs of some of their learners. In the last section, *Language and Representation,* teachers share how they help students use representations and develop language to investigate and express mathematical ideas. The questions at the end of each case provide a starting point for your own reflection or for discussion with colleagues. See *Implementing Investigations in Grade 5* for this set of episodes.

Mathematical Emphases

The Base-Ten Number System Extending knowledge of the number system to 100,000 and beyond

Math Focus Points

◆ Reading, writing, and sequencing numbers to 10,000 and 100,000

◆ Understanding the place-value relationships between 10, 100, 1,000, and 10,000

◆ Learning the names of places larger than 100,000: million, billion, trillion

Computational Fluency Adding and subtracting accurately and efficiently

Math Focus Points

◆ Adding and subtracting multiples of 100 and 1,000

◆ Finding the difference between a number and 10,000

◆ Finding combinations of 3-digit numbers that add to 1,000

◆ Solving addition and subtraction problems with large numbers by focusing on the place value of the digits

This Investigation also focuses on

◆ Using story contexts and representations, such as number lines, to explain and justify solutions to subtraction problems

Using Place Values

	Student Activity Book	Student Math Handbook	Professional Development: Read Ahead of Time	
SESSION 1.1 p. 26				
Working with the 10,000 Chart Students learn a new Ten-Minute Math activity, *Practicing Place Value.* Then they use a chart of 10,000 squares to study the place-value structure of numbers in the thousands.	1	6	• **Mathematics in This Unit,** p. 10 • **Part 4: Ten-Minute Math** in *Implementing Investigations in Grade 5:* Practicing Place Value • **Teacher Note:** Addition Strategies, p. 116	
SESSION 1.2 p. 32				
Assessment: Numbers on the 10,000 Chart Students study the place-value structure of numbers in the thousands as they add and subtract multiples of 100 and write the numbers on their 10,000 charts. Students are assessed on their ability to read, write and sequence numbers up to 10,000.	2–5	6		
SESSION 1.3 p. 36				
How Many Steps to 10,000? Students continue interpreting place value as they add and subtract. Students find the distance from a given number to 10,000 and find sums of 3-digit numbers as close to 1,000 as possible.	7–11	G2	• **Teacher Note:** Representing Subtraction on the Number Line, p. 118 • **Dialogue Box:** How Many Steps to 10,000?, p. 142	
SESSION 1.4 p. 43				
Adding and Subtracting Large Numbers Students review multiplication with the new Ten-Minute Math activity, *Estimation and Number Sense: Closest Estimate.* They also solve sets of related addition and subtraction problems in which they use their knowledge of place-value relationships.	2–3, 13–17	G2	• **Algebra Connections in This Unit,** p. 16 • **Part 4: Ten-Minute Math** in *Implementing Investigations in Grade 5:* Estimation and Number Sense: Closest Estimate	
SESSION 1.5 p. 51				
Adding and Subtracting Large Numbers, *continued* Students use multiples of 10, 100, and 1,000 (landmark numbers) and place-value relationships to solve addition and subtraction problems with large numbers.	2–3, 13–15, 19	6, 7; G2		

Materials to Gather	Materials to Prepare
• **Fine-tipped erasable markers** (2 per group)	• **10,000 charts** Tape over "10,000" on the charts until students determine the number of squares. Decide where students will work on these: taped to the wall, on the floor, spread across several desks, or on tables. Make space available as necessary. (1 per group) • **M1–M2, Family Letter** Make copies. (1 per student)
• **10,000 charts** (1 per group; from Session 1.1) • **Fine-tipped erasable markers** (2 per group)	• **M3, Assessment Checklist: Numbers to 100,000** ✓ Make copies. (several per class)
• **T35, *Close to 1,000* Recording Sheet** 🖳 • **10,000 charts** (1 per group; from Session 1.1) • **Fine-tipped erasable markers** (2 per group)	• **M4–M6, Digit Cards** If you are not using manufactured Digit Cards, make copies and cut apart, or reuse the decks of cards from Unit 1. (1 deck per pair) • **M8, *Close to 1,000*** Make copies. (as needed) • **M9–M10, Family Letter** Make copies. (1 per student) • **T21–T23, Digit Cards** 🖳 Cut apart and store in an envelope or plastic sleeve in the Resources Binder if this was not already done in Unit 1.
• **Digit Cards** (1 deck per pair; from Session 1.3) • **M8, *Close to 1,000*** (as needed; from Session 1.3) • **T36, *Estimation and Number Sense: Closest Estimate*** 🖳 (page 1 of 3) • **10,000 charts** (1 per group; from Session 1.1) • **Fine-tipped erasable markers** (2 per group)	• **M7, *Close to 1,000* Recording Sheet** Make copies. (as needed)
• **Digit Cards** (1 deck per pair; from Session 1.3) • **M7, *Close to 1,000* Recording Sheet** (as needed; from Session 1.4) • **M8, *Close to 1,000*** (as needed; from Session 1.3) • **10,000 charts** (1 per group; from Session 1.1) • **Fine-tipped erasable markers** (2 per group)	

🖳 Overhead Transparency   ✓ Checklist Available

Working with the 10,000 Chart

Math Focus Points

◆ Reading, writing, and sequencing numbers to 10,000 and 100,000

◆ Understanding the place-value relationships between 10, 100, 1,000, and 10,000

Today's Plan		Materials
ACTIVITY ➊ Practicing Place Value	🕐 15 MIN 👥 CLASS	
ACTIVITY ➋ Introducing the 10,000 Chart	🕐 15 MIN 👥 CLASS 👥 GROUPS	• 10,000 charts*; fine-tipped erasable markers
ACTIVITY ➌ Numbers on the 10,000 Chart	🕐 30 MIN 👥 GROUPS	• 10,000 charts; fine-tipped erasable markers (2 per group)
SESSION FOLLOW-UP ➍ Daily Practice		• *Student Activity Book*, p. 1 • *Student Math Handbook*, p. 6 • M1–M2, Family Letter*

*See *Materials to Prepare*, p. 25.

Ten-Minute Math

NOTE: The Ten-Minute Math activity for this unit, *Practicing Place Value*, is introduced in this session. Plan to do today's Ten-Minute Math sometime after math class, or if it is not possible, choose a Ten-Minute Math activity from a previous unit, such as *Estimation and Number Sense*, with which your students are familiar.

Practicing Place Value   Write 7,805 on the board and have students practice saying it. Make sure all students can read, write, and say this number correctly. Ask students to solve these problems mentally, if possible:

• What is 7,805 + 2,000? 7,805 + 5,000? 7,805 − 3,000? 7,805 + 200? 7,805 − 300? Which places have the same digits? Which do not? Why?

Write each answer on the board. Ask students to compare each sum or difference with 7,805. If time remains, pose additional similar problems using these numbers: 6,031 and 7,492.

ACTIVITY

1 Practicing Place Value

15 MIN   CLASS

Professional Development

❶ **Part 4: Ten-Minute Math** in *Implementing Investigations in Grade 5:* Practicing Place Value

Introduce the new unit by explaining to students that for the next few weeks they are going to be studying place value and adding and subtracting large numbers. Have students use either blank paper or math journals for this activity.

Today, we're going to start a new Ten-Minute Math activity called *Practicing Place Value.*❶ We'll continue doing this activity throughout the unit.

On the board, write this number: 8,435.

Turn to your neighbor and say this number . . . Who will read the number for us?

Accept either "eight thousand, four hundred, thirty-five" or "eighty-four hundred, thirty five."

Next to 8,435, write: + 5,000.

On your paper, write the sum. Then read the new number to your neighbor to make sure you both agree.

Ask a student volunteer to come to the board to write and read the new number.

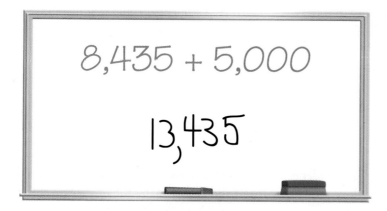

Ask the student at the board, or the whole class, the following questions:

* How did you decide what the sum is?

* What is the value of each digit in the sum?

* Compare 8,435 to the sum, 13,435. In which places are the digits the same?

* Which are different? Why?

Teaching Notes

❷ **Managing Space with the 10,000 Charts** These charts take up a lot of space. Students may work on them either taped to a wall, on the floor, or spread across several desks or a table. You might need to clear off a wall of your classroom or perhaps use another space in the school (e.g., the gym). Although the charts can be cumbersome, the discussion students have with each other, and with the teacher, is important. The charts provide a very useful visual image of the size of numbers in the thousands.

❸ **Place Value and the 10,000 Chart** The purpose of using this 10,000 chart is for students to see what 10,000 looks like as a quantity, and to see how 10,000 is composed of 100 groups (rows) of 100, and 10 groups (rectangles) of 1,000. As you work with students on this chart and throughout the unit, continually focus on these aspects of place value. When students have completed the 10,000 chart activities, post several of the charts in the room for the remainder of the unit so that students can refer to the charts, and use them as necessary.

Professional Development

❹ **Teacher Note:** Place Value, p. 113

Differentiation

❺ **English Language Learners** In this activity, English Language Learners need to understand the vocabulary of estimation and logical reasoning. You may want to review appropriate terminology with them ahead of time. Spread a variety of multi-colored shapes or objects on the table and ask, "*About* how many of the shapes are red? Let's just make a *guess*, or *estimate*. Now, let's see *exactly* how many red shapes there are. How can we get an *exact* number?" Once the students have answered your questions, have them explain how they got their answers. Encourage them to use similar strategies while working on this activity.

Use the following numbers and problems, as time permits:

4,987	16,234
4,987 + 3,000	16,234 + 1,000
4,987 − 500	16,234 + 10,000
4,987 − 1,000	16,234 − 10,000

ONGOING ASSESSMENT: Observing Students at Work

Students read and write large numbers. They add and subtract multiples of 10, 100, and 1,000.

- **Are students able to read and write large numbers correctly?** If not, with which numbers do they have difficulty?

- **Are students able to easily add and subtract multiples of 100 and 1,000?**

ACTIVITY

15 MIN   CLASS   GROUPS

❷ Introducing the 10,000 Chart

Distribute or post one chart for each group,❷ but do not to call them "10,000 charts" since students will be figuring out how many squares are in the chart.❸ ❹ To help students begin thinking about the structure of the chart, ask them to consider the following questions in their small groups:

- Just by looking at the chart, about how many squares do you think are on these charts? Why?

- Can you figure out exactly how many squares are on the chart? How do you know?❺

Give students 5 minutes to discuss these questions, and then have a whole group discussion about how many squares are on the chart, eliciting student ideas about how they figured it out.

Students might say:

"We counted 100 in each row. Then we counted by 100s. When we got to 1,000 we saw that it was one rectangle. Then we counted the rectangles by 1,000s."

"We think there are 10,000 squares, because we counted 100 rows across and 100 rows down and we knew that 100 × 100 = 10,000."

"We agree there are 10,000, but we found there were 1,000 squares in one of the rectangles, and there are 10 rectangles. 1,000 × 10 = 10,000."

Now ask students to visualize numbering each square of the chart, from 1 to 10,000. Ask questions like the following:

- What would happen if we numbered every square from 1 to 10,000, going all the way across the first row, then starting at the beginning of the second row and numbering all the way across, and so forth?

- What number should go in the first square in the upper left hand corner?

- What number should go in the very last square, in the bottom right hand corner?

Have students write in a "1" in the first square and "10,000" in the last square.

About where would you expect 50 to go? About where would you expect 100 to go?

Ask just enough questions to orient students to how the chart will be numbered. Students worked on a 10,000 chart in Grade 4, but that chart was put together from a hundred 100 charts, with the numbering from 1–100, 101–200, 201–300, and so forth, within each individual 100 chart. Therefore, they may need a few minutes to visualize how this chart will be numbered.

Now introduce the idea of choosing some numbers to put on the chart in such a way that these numbers will help them find the squares for other numbers on the chart.

Suppose you want to easily find the square for a particular number. We could write in every number, but that would take a long time. So each group is going to decide on some landmark numbers—numbers

⑥ Landmark Multiples In one classroom, students wrote all the multiples of 100, and then every number that ended in 50. In another classroom, students used some, but not all of the numbers that ended in 25, 50, or 00.

that you feel are important so you can quickly find the number for any square on your chart. Talk to your group. What are some landmark numbers everyone should write on their charts? Don't write any numbers yet; just talk about what numbers will be helpful.

Give students several minutes to discuss this.

What are some landmark numbers we should list?

Listen to suggestions, ask if the class agrees, and record students' responses on the board.⑥

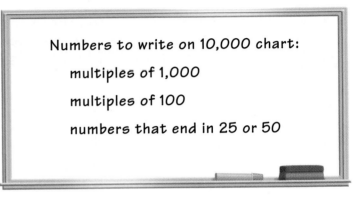

Numbers to write on 10,000 chart:

multiples of 1,000

multiples of 100

numbers that end in 25 or 50

For each set of numbers that students suggest, ask them how many numbers they would have to write. (For example, there are 100 multiples of 100. There are 200 numbers that end in 25 or 50.)

ACTIVITY

③ Numbers on the 10,000 Chart

30 MIN   GROUPS

Students have the rest of the session and part of the next session to write numbers on their charts.

Students write landmark numbers on the 10,000 chart to help them easily locate the squares for other numbers.

As students are working, circulate and ask questions to help them think about the structure of the chart. This is a good time for you to do an informal assessment of your students' understanding of reading, writing, and sequencing numbers up to 10,000.

Where would 1,223 be on your chart? How do you know?

Point to one of the numbers they have written, such as 3,750.

What number would be one row below 3,750? [the number plus 100]

Three rows below? [the number plus 300] How many rows above this would 3,550 be? [2] How do you know?

Students will have additional time in Session 1.2 to write numbers on their charts. Once groups have labeled some of the landmark numbers, it will be useful to use those same charts again throughout the Investigation. Tell students they should not wipe the chart clean at the end of each session. As the Investigation progresses, have students work in the same groups with the same chart they were given today.

ONGOING ASSESSMENT: Observing Students at Work ✔

Students locate and write numbers on the 10,000 chart.

- **How do students know where to write the number?** What landmarks are they using?

- **Are students using the structure of the chart to help them locate numbers?** Do they recognize that each row is 100 squares? Do they realize that 1,250 would be closer to the top of the chart, and 8,250 would be closer to the bottom?

- **Do any students have difficulty reading or writing these numbers?**

SESSION FOLLOW-UP

4 Daily Practice

 Daily Practice: For reinforcement of this unit's content, have students complete *Student Activity Book* page 1.

 Student Math Handbook: Students and families may use *Student Math Handbook* page 6 for reference and review. See pages 149–151 in the back of this unit.

Family Letter: Send home copies of the Family Letter (M1–M2).

Name _____ Date _____
Thousands of Miles, Thousands of Seats   Daily Practice

Addition and Subtraction Problems

NOTE Students solve addition and subtraction problems in which multiples of 10, 100, and 1,000 are added to and subtracted from 4-digit numbers.
6

1. 3,267 + 10 = _____   2. 3,267 – 10 = _____
3. 3,267 + 50 = _____   4. 3,267 – 50 = _____
5. 3,267 + 100 = _____   6. 3,267 – 100 = _____
7. 3,267 + 500 = _____   8. 3,267 – 500 = _____
9. 9,702 – 10 = _____   10. 9,702 + 300 = _____
11. 9,702 – 20 = _____   12. 9,702 + 500 = _____
13. 9,702 – 200 = _____   14. 9,702 + 5,000 = _____
15. 9,702 – 2,000 = _____ 16. 9,702 + 10,000 = _____

17. Choose one of the above problems, and explain how you found the answer.

Ongoing Review

18. 8,003 – 600 = _____

A. 5,003   B. 7,400   C. 7,403   D. 8,403

Session 1.1   Unit 3   1

▲ **Student Activity Book, p. 1**

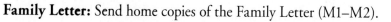

Assessment: Numbers on the 10,000 Chart

Math Focus Points

◈ Reading, writing, and sequencing numbers to 10,000 and 100,000

◈ Understanding the place-value relationships between 10, 100, 1,000, and 10,000

◈ Adding and subtracting multiples of 100 and 1,000

Today's Plan		Materials
① ASSESSMENT ACTIVITY **Numbers on the 10,000 Chart**	15 MIN GROUPS	• M3* ☑ • 10,000 charts (from Session 1.1); fine-tipped erasable markers
② ACTIVITY **Introducing Moving Up and Down the Chart**	15 MIN CLASS GROUPS	• 10,000 charts (from Session 1.1); fine-tipped erasable markers
③ ACTIVITY **Adding and Subtracting Multiples of 100**	30 MIN GROUPS	• *Student Activity Book*, pp. 2–3 • 10,000 charts (from Session 1.1); fine-tipped erasable markers
④ SESSION FOLLOW-UP **Daily Practice and Homework**		• *Student Activity Book*, pp. 4–5 • *Student Math Handbook*, p. 6

*See *Materials to Prepare*, p. 25.

Ten-Minute Math

Practicing Place Value Write 6,830 on the board and have students practice saying it. Make sure all students can read, write, and say this number correctly. Ask students to solve these problems mentally, if possible:

• What is 6,830 + 5,000? 6,830 + 10,000? 6,830 − 3,000? 6,830 + 400? 6,830 − 300?

Write each answer on the board. Ask students to compare each sum or difference with 6,830.

Which places have the same digits? Which do not? Why?

If time remains, pose additional similar problems using these numbers: 8,419 and 7,007.

ASSESSMENT ACTIVITY
1 Numbers on the 10,000 Chart

15 MIN GROUPS

Give students an additional 15 minutes to write more numbers on their 10,000 charts. See Session 1.1, pages 30–31, for a full description of this activity. Students who have not finished can continue to fill in more numbers at other times during the school day or when they have completed other work.

This session includes an observed assessment of Benchmark 1: Read, write, and sequence numbers up to 100,000. However, in this session you are assessing students' work with numbers up to 10,000. As students continue to fill out their 10,000 charts and to move up and down the chart in the following two activities, check in with each student for about a minute. Ask each student to do the following:

• Read two or three numbers on the 10,000 chart

• Write two or three numbers in the thousands

Answer two or three questions about sequence, such as "What is the number that is one less than the one you just read? What about 1 more? What about 10 less? 100 less?" ❶

DIFFERENTIATION: Supporting the Range of Learners

ELL English Language Learner Before this activity, you may need to review the meaning of *sequence* and similar words, such as *series* and order. You can also visually demonstrate sequence-related words such as more, *less, above,* and *below.* Using number cards, lay a selection of numbers (1–10, 11–20, 75–100, etc.) out of sequence on the table. Ask, "Can you help me put these cards in *order?*" Once students have completed the task, ask questions about sequence. "Which number is two *more* than the first number? Which number is one *less* than the last number? Is the number (16) *above* or *below* the number (14)? Which numbers are *below* the number (12)? Which numbers are *above* this number?"

ACTIVITY
2 Introducing Moving Up and Down the Chart

15 MIN CLASS GROUPS

Students practice reading, writing, and sequencing numbers by locating more numbers on the 10,000 chart. They continue to explore the meaning

Teaching Note

❶ **Assessment Checklist** Use the first half of Assessment Checklist: Numbers to 100,000 (M3) to record student responses. You will use the second half of the checklist when you assess student's ability to read, write, and sequence numbers to 100,000 in Session 3.3.

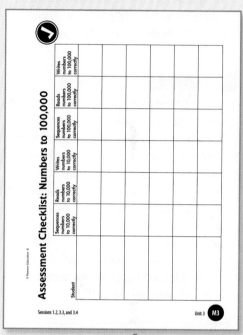

▲ **Resource Masters, M3** ✓

Math Note

❷ "Above" and "Below" on the 10,000 Chart In their work with the 10,000 chart, students answer questions such as "What number is 4 rows above 750? What number is 12 rows below 750?" In this activity, "above" or "below" means directly above or directly below in the same column. For example, the number 4 rows above 750 on the 10,000 chart is 350, and the number 12 rows below 750 is 1,950. Usually students have no trouble understanding this convention.

Teaching Note

❸ Moving Around on the Chart Help students notice and articulate that numbers increase from left to right and from the top to the bottom of the chart. Numbers decrease from right to left and from the bottom to the top of the chart. Be careful about using phrases like "numbers going up" to mean that numbers are getting larger, as some students may hear "up" as moving upwards on the chart. While students are getting used to this chart, keep asking questions such as: "If you add 100 (200, 500) to this number, where will you land? If you subtract 100 (200, 500), where will you land?"

Numbers on the 10,000 Chart (page 1 of 2)

1. Label these squares on the 10,000 chart:

9,970	3,770	1,508	5,020	8,854
7,305	2,965	6,351	7,642	2,020
9,033	4,139	1,215	3,290	6,897
4,786	115	490	8,460	5,645

In Problems 2–16, find each number described below, and write the equation that shows the addition or subtraction. Label the new square on the 10,000 chart. Work with your small group on this, but each of you should complete these pages.

Example:
What number is 3 rows below 1,250? __1,550__
Equation: __1,250 + 300 = 1,550__

What number is:
2. 1 row below 750? _____   Equation: _____
3. 5 rows below 750? _____   Equation: _____
4. 12 rows below 750? _____   Equation: _____
5. 4 rows above 750? _____   Equation: _____
6. 40 rows below 750? _____   Equation: _____

2 Unit 3   Sessions 1.2, 1.4, 1.5

▲ **Student Activity Book, pp. 2–3**

---

of the place-value notation by adding and subtracting, using the chart.

Have everyone find 1,250 on their 10,000 chart.

What number is 5 rows below 1,250? Talk to another member of your group, and locate the new number on the chart.

Encourage students to notice how the structure of the chart is related to adding (or subtracting). For example, moving down 5 rows models adding 500.

Ask a student to say the new number (1,750) and ask how they knew. On the board, write: $1,250 + 500 = 1,750$.

Go back to 1,250. How many rows above that number is 950?❷ Talk to another member of your group.

Ask a student to say how many rows (3) and ask how they knew. On the board, write: $1,250 - 300 = 950$.

Go back to 1,250. What number is 75 more? Talk to another member of your group, and point to the new number.❸

Ask a student to say the new number (1,325), and write on the board: $1,250 + 75 = 1,325$.

Adding 75 is not as simple as going up or down rows. You might want to call on more than one student to hear their strategies.

Students might say:

"I added 50 and got 1,300, then added 25 more and got 1,325."

"I went down one row and that was 1,350, then I went back 25 to 1,325."

ACTIVITY

③ Adding and Subtracting Multiples of 100

30 MIN   GROUPS

Students complete *Student Activity Book* pages 2 and 3. Students may work in their groups of 3 or 5, but each student completes the pages individually. Since there is a great deal of work on these pages, the activity may take longer than suggested. In that case, students can complete this as an additional activity in the Math Workshop in Sessions 1.4 and 1.5.

Give students about 15 minutes to work, and then call them back together briefly to discuss what they are noting about the structure of the chart.

How does the structure of the chart help you answer these problems? What was easy? What was hard? . . . [Walter] thinks counting by 100s is easy because you just move up or down the same column. Any thoughts?

Students use the remainder of the session to work on pages 2 and 3. ❹ If students seem to be having difficulty, consider doing a few more examples with the class, or working with smaller groups of students.

ONGOING ASSESSMENT: Observing Students at Work

Students locate numbers on the 10,000 chart and add and subtract multiples of 100.

- **Are students using relationships on the chart to locate numbers?** Do they go to the right location on the chart (e.g., if the number is 1,250, do they know to look in the second large rectangle and not look at the bottom of the chart?)

- **Do students understand the structure of the chart?** Do they know that one row is 100, that numbers get larger as you go down the chart, and so on?

- **Are students fluent in adding and subtracting multiples of 100?**

SESSION FOLLOW-UP

4 Daily Practice and Homework

 Daily Practice: For ongoing review, have students complete *Student Activity Book* page 4.

 Homework: Students practice solving 4-digit addition problems on *Student Activity Book* page 5. ❺ ❻

 Student Math Handbook: Students and families may use *Student Math Handbook* page 6 for reference and review. See pages 149–151 in the back of this unit.

Teaching Notes

❹ **Making Certain Students Use the Chart** As students complete *Student Activity Book* pages 2–3, many students will be able to do the problems mentally, adding and subtracting multiples of 100. This is an important skill all students should be using. It is also important, however, that they locate these numbers on the 10,000 chart. Teachers report that many students are able to solve the problems mentally, but then cannot find the numbers on the chart. This activity provides practice in both adding and subtracting multiples of 100, and on place-value relationships, including the relative size of quantities.

❺ **Addition Strategies** It is expected that students come to Grade 5 able to fluently solve addition problems. This homework provides review and practice of students' addition strategies.

Professional Development

❻ **Teacher Note:** Addition Strategies, p. 116

▲ **Student Activity Book, pp. 4–5**

How Many Steps to 10,000?

Math Focus Points

◆ Finding the difference between a number and 10,000

◆ Finding combinations of 3-digit numbers that add to 1,000

◆ Using story contexts and representations, such as number lines, to explain and justify solutions to subtraction problems

Today's Plan		Materials
ACTIVITY **①** **Introducing How Many Steps to 10,000?**	15 MIN · CLASS · GROUPS	• 10,000 charts (from Session 1.1); fine-tipped erasable markers
ACTIVITY **②** **How Many Steps to 10,000?**	25 MIN · INDIVIDUALS	• *Student Activity Book,* pp. 7–8 • 10,000 charts (from Session 1.1)
ACTIVITY **③** *Close to 1,000*	20 MIN · CLASS · PAIRS	• *Student Activity Book,* p. 9 • M4–M6 (from Unit 1)*; M8* (as needed); T21–T23*; T35
SESSION FOLLOW-UP **④** **Daily Practice and Homework**		• *Student Activity Book,* pp. 10–11 • *Student Math Handbook,* p. G2 • M9–M10, Family Letter*

*See *Materials to Prepare,* p. 25.

Ten-Minute Math

Practicing Place Value Say "thirteen thousand, one hundred two" and have students write the number. Make sure all students can read, write, and say this number correctly. Ask students to solve these problems mentally, if possible:

- What is $13,102 + 4,000$? $13,102 + 400$? $13,102 - 4,000$? $13,102 - 400$? $13,102 - 900$? Which places have the same digits? Which do not? Why?

Write each answer on the board. Ask students to compare each sum or difference with 13,102. If time remains, pose additional similar problems using these numbers: 19,008 and 17,091.

ACTIVITY

Introducing How Many Steps to 10,000?

15 MIN   CLASS   GROUPS

Students continue interpreting place value in order to add and subtract by finding the distance from given numbers to 10,000 on the 10,000 chart. Ask students to imagine the 10,000 chart as a giant game board.❶ If there is a game you know your students play that involves moving a game marker by steps along a board, you might refer to that game.

Imagine that a tiny creature is moving along this board. It starts at the edge of the board, in the upper left corner, steps onto the first square and moves across a whole row to 100, stepping on every square. So to get to 100, it takes 100 steps. Then it jumps to the beginning of the next row, to 101, moves across that whole row, and so forth. It always moves one square at a time. We'll count each square the creature moves across as a step. Sometimes it moves backwards. You're going to be solving problems about how many steps it would take to move from a particular square to the end of the board.

Let's say the creature is on the square numbered 1,025. Find that square on the 10,000 chart. Then figure out how many steps it would have to take to get to the 10,000th square.❷

Give groups a few minutes to do this and then ask several students to explain their thinking. As you collect answers, it is important to model different ways to represent the solutions both with notation and on a number line. It is not expected that students use all the different notations, but it is important that students see these different notations and develop their own clear notation.

You might want to remind students of the work they did with number lines in Grades 3 and 4, both as a tool for solving problems, and as a way to represent their thinking. The number line is a way for students to visualize the difference between two numbers and can be an important tool for some students to use for solving distance problems, along with the 10,000 chart.❸

Professional Development

❶ **Dialogue Box:** How Many Steps to 10,000?, p. 142

Algebra Note

❷ **The Relationship Between Addition and Subtraction**   It is likely that many students solve these problems by adding up to 10,000 ($1{,}025 +$ _____ $= 10{,}000$), and others solve it using subtraction ($10{,}000 -$ _____ $= 1{,}025$). Find opportunities to call attention to this relationship as students share their solutions. For more information about the inverse relationship between addition and subtraction, see "Algebra Connections in This Unit" on page 16.

Professional Development

❸ **Teacher Note:** Representing Subtraction on the Number Line, p. 118

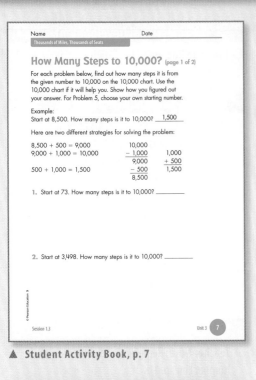

How Many Steps to 10,000? (page 1 of 2)

For each problem below, find out how many steps it is from the given number to 10,000 on the 10,000 chart. Use the 10,000 chart if it will help you. Show how you figured out your answer. For Problem 5, choose your own starting number.

Example:
Start at 8,500. How many steps is it to 10,000? ___1,500___

Here are two different strategies for solving the problem:

8,500 + 500 = 9,000
9,000 + 1,000 = 10,000
500 + 1,000 = 1,500

1. Start at 73. How many steps is it to 10,000? _____

2. Start at 3,498. How many steps is it to 10,000? _____

▲ Student Activity Book, p. 7

Math Note

❹ Using the Equal Sign Correctly As students are working, check to be certain they are using correct notation for their answers. Sometimes students record their solutions using several equal signs strung together like this: $1,025 + 8,000 = 9,025 + 900 = 9,925 + 75 = 10,000$. This is incorrect because those expressions are not all equal to each other (e.g., $1,025 + 8,000$ is not equal to $9,025 + 900$). These steps should be written as separate equations:

$1,025 + 8,000 = 9,025$

$9,025 + 900 = 9,925$

$9,925 + 75 = 10,000$

Many fifth graders should be able to carry out some of these steps mentally. As the unit continues, help students choose which steps they need to record in order to keep track of their work.

---

② How Many Steps to 10,000?

Remind students that the 10,000 charts or a number line are useful tools to help solve the problems on *Student Activity Book* pages 7–8. Each student completes pages 7–8 individually, but students will need to share the 10,000 charts.❹

Students find how many steps it is from given numbers to 10,000 using tools such as the 10,000 chart, number lines, and various computational strategies.

ONGOING ASSESSMENT: Observing Students at Work

Students find the difference between a given number and 10,000.

- **How do students find the difference?** Are they adding or subtracting large chunks of numbers? Are they using landmarks?

- **Are students using correct notation to show their answers?**

- **Can students carry out some steps mentally?**

As you observe students working, consider the variety of strategies that students use. Look for students who use the 10,000 chart, or another representation such as a number line. Ask them to show you the "stopping off places" they use as they add up or subtract back.

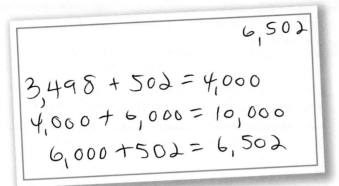

6,502

3,498 + 502 = 4,000

4,000 + 6,000 = 10,000

6,000 + 502 = 6,502

Sample Student Work

1,994

8,006 + 1,000 = 9,006

9,006 + 900 = 9,906

9,906 + 90 = 9,996

9,996 + 4 = 10,000

Sample Student Work

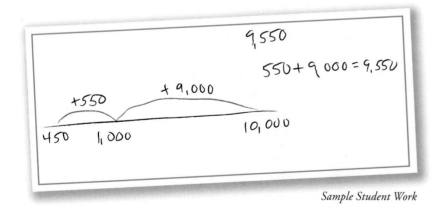

9,550

550 + 9,000 = 9,550

+550   + 9,000

450   1,000   10,000

Sample Student Work

Name _____ Date _____

Thousands of Miles, Thousands of Seats

How Many Steps to 10,000? (page 2 of 2)

3. Start at 8,006. How many steps is it to 10,000? _____

4. Start at 450. How many steps is it to 10,000? _____

5. Start at _____. How many steps is it to 10,000? _____

8   Unit 3   Session 1.3

▲ **Student Activity Book, p. 8**

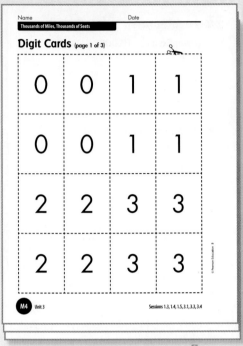

Name _____ Date _____

Thousands of Miles, Thousands of Seats

Digit Cards (page 1 of 3) ✂

0	0	1	1
0	0	1	1
2	2	3	3
2	2	3	3

M4 Unit 3   Sessions 1.3, 1.4, 1.5, 3.1, 3.3, 3.4

▲ **Resource Masters, M4–M6; T21–T23**

Name _____ Date _____

Thousands of Miles, Thousands of Seats

Close to 1,000 Recording Sheet

Game 1   Score
Round 1:
___ ___ + ___ ___ = ___   ___
Round 2:
___ ___ + ___ ___ = ___   ___
Round 3:
___ ___ + ___ ___ = ___   ___
Round 4:
___ ___ + ___ ___ = ___   ___
Round 5:
___ ___ + ___ ___ = ___   ___
                              Final Score: ___

Game 2   Score
Round 1:
___ ___ + ___ ___ = ___   ___
Round 2:
___ ___ + ___ ___ = ___   ___
Round 3:
___ ___ + ___ ___ = ___   ___
Round 4:
___ ___ + ___ ___ = ___   ___
Round 5:
___ ___ + ___ ___ = ___   ___
                              Final Score: ___

Sessions 1.3–1.5   Unit 3 9

▲ **Student Activity Book, p. 9;**
Resource Masters, M7; T35

DIFFERENTIATION: Supporting the Range of Learners

Intervention Some students may struggle with the size of the numbers and may not be using multiples of hundreds or thousands in their computation. These students should be using the 10,000 charts to solve the problems and will benefit from working with numbers that are multiples of thousands, or with landmark numbers like 2,500, or 4,500. Ask questions such as the following:

● How far is it from 2,000 to 10,000? From 7,000 to 10,000? From 2,500 to 10,000?

You may want to work with a small group of these students during the Math Workshop in Sessions 1.4 and 1.5.

ACTIVITY

3

20 MIN CLASS PAIRS

Close to 1,000

Bring students back together, even though some may still be working on *Student Activity Book* pages 7–8, to reacquaint the class with *Close to 1,000*. In this game, which students played in Grade 4, students find combinations of two numbers that add up to 1,000. Make available copies of the game rules, *Close to 1,000* (M8).

Does anyone remember playing Close to 1,000? It was a game that you learned in fourth grade. Can someone tell us how it's played?

As one or two students describe the directions, demonstrate on the overhead using the transparent Digit Cards (T21–T23) or by drawing the cards on the board. The game is played by drawing eight cards and using six of them to make two 3-digit numbers that, when added together, have a sum that is as close to 1,000 as possible. Draw eight cards and show them to the students.

How would you use these cards to make two 3-digit numbers with a sum of exactly 1,000, or as close to 1,000 as you can get? What size numbers are you going to be looking for? Remember that it's OK to go over 1,000. Your score is going to be the difference between the sum and 1,000, whether the sum is greater than, or less than, 1,000.

Give students a few minutes to talk to a partner about the problem, and then take suggestions. Record each suggestion that is offered, and for each suggestion, ask the students whether or not they have come as close as they can. When the class has decided that they have made an addition combination that comes the closest, write it on a transparency of the

Close to 1,000 Recording Sheet (T35), along with the sum. Then ask what the difference would be between the sum and 1,000, and write that in the space marked "Score."

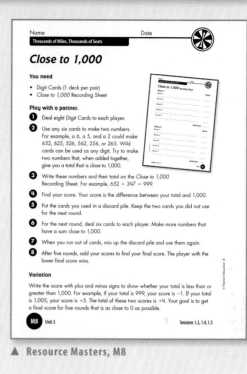

▲ Resource Masters, M8

In Close to 1,000, *players practice adding 3-digit numbers to make sums that are close to 1,000.*

Remind students that they play five rounds and then add up their scores. They keep track of the rounds on *Student Activity Book* page 9. The player with the lowest final score wins the game. If some students are unsure about how to play the game, play a few more rounds either with the whole class or with the group of students who have questions, and then have students play the game in pairs.

Tell students to begin focusing on strategies they use to play *Close to 1,000*.

As you're playing *Close to 1,000* with your partner, think about what mental strategies you're using to add numbers that equal 1,000, or close to it. What combinations that equal 1,000 do you already know? How do you decide what digits go in the hundreds, tens, or ones places as you make your numbers?

ONGOING ASSESSMENT: Observing Students at Work

Students create two 3-digit numbers with a sum as close to 1,000 as possible.

- **Are students considering the value of the digits in each place of the numbers they make?** Do they try to make a sum of 9 in the hundreds place and in the tens place and a sum of 10 in the ones place?

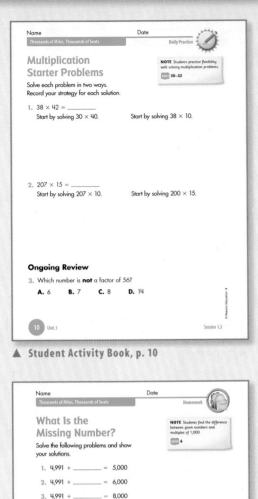

▲ **Student Activity Book, p. 10**

▲ **Student Activity Book, p. 11**

- **Do they use known combinations such as 400 + 600, or 250 + 750?** Or are they creating any 3-digit numbers and adding them to see how close they are to 1,000? How do they adjust a combination they've tried in order to get closer to 1,000?

- **What strategies do students use to find the difference between their sum and 1,000?** Do they add up from their sum to 1,000, or do they create subtraction problems? If their sums have gone over 1,000, can they use a mental strategy to find the difference?

DIFFERENTIATION: Supporting the Range of Learners

Intervention If there are students who have trouble getting started with this game, help them think about what combinations they see in the cards that could be a starting place. Are there landmark numbers that might be helpful? You can also choose a number for them to start with and ask them what number could be added to make the sum exactly 1,000.

Extension Students who easily play the game should play with the scoring variation of using positive and negative numbers.

SESSION FOLLOW-UP

4 Daily Practice and Homework

Daily Practice: For ongoing review, have students complete *Student Activity Book* page 10.

Homework: Students find the difference between given numbers and multiples of 1,000 on *Student Activity Book* page 11.

Student Math Handbook: Students and families may use *Student Math Handbook* page G2 for reference and review. See pages 149–151 in the back of this unit.

Family Letter: Send home copies of the Family Letter (M9–M10).

Adding and Subtracting Large Numbers

Math Focus Points

◆ Solving addition and subtraction problems with large numbers by focusing on the place value of the digits

◆ Finding the difference between a number and 10,000

◆ Finding combinations of 3-digit numbers that add to 1,000

Today's Plan		Materials
① ACTIVITY **Introducing** *Estimation and Number Sense: Closest Estimate*	10 MIN CLASS	• T36
② ACTIVITY **Related Problems**	25 MIN CLASS	
③ MATH WORKSHOP **Adding and Subtracting Large Numbers** **3A** Adding and Subtracting Multiples of 100 **3B** Related Problems **3C** How Many Steps to 10,000? **3D** *Close to 1,000*	25 MIN	**3A** • Materials from Session 1.2, p. 32 **3B** • *Student Activity Book,* pp. 13–15 **3C** • Materials from Session 1.3, p. 36 **3D** • Digit Cards (from Session 1.3); M7 (as needed)*; M8 (as needed; from Session 1.3)
④ SESSION FOLLOW-UP **Daily Practice and Homework**		• *Student Activity Book,* pp. 16–17 • *Student Math Handbook,* p. G2

*See *Materials to Prepare,* p. 25.

Ten-Minute Math

Practicing Place Value Say "forty-six thousand, forty-nine" and have students write the number. Ask students to solve these problems mentally, if possible:

• What is 46,049 + 3,000? 46,049 + 5,000? 46,049 + 500? 46,049 − 3,000? 46,049 − 8,000? Which places have the same digits? Which do not? Why?

Write each answer on the board. Ask students to compare each sum or difference with 46,049.

Professional Development

❶ **Part 4: Ten-Minute Math** in *Implementing Investigations in Grade 5:* Estimation and Number Sense: Closest Estimate

---

Thousands of Miles, Thousands of Seats

Estimation and Number Sense: Closest Estimate (page 1 of 3)

1. $42 \times 18 \approx$	420	800	840
2. $67 \times 45 \approx$	280	2,800	28,000
3. $56 \times 72 \approx$	3,500	4,000	4,200
4. $362 \div 3 \approx$	12	120	1,200
5. $893 \div 4 \approx$	22	200	225
6. $550 \div 7 \approx$	80	90	100

© Pearson Education 5

T36

▲ Transparencies, T36

ACTIVITY

10 MIN   CLASS

① Introducing *Estimation and Number Sense: Closest Estimate*

Students learn a variation of the Ten-Minute Math activity, *Estimation and Number Sense: Closest Estimate.*

We're going to start a new Ten-Minute Math activity today. It's called *Closest Estimate.*❶ In this unit, we're going to practice finding the closest estimate for multiplication and division problems. I'll show you a problem for 15 seconds or so, and your job is to choose the closest estimate. Don't try to find the exact answer, just an estimate. I also want you to think about whether the closest estimate is greater than or less than the actual answer. Let's try one.

Show Problem 1 (42×18) from the transparency *Estimation and Number Sense: Closest Estimate* (T36) (page 1 of 3).

1. $42 \times 18 \approx$ 420   800   840

If students are unfamiliar with the $\approx$ sign, tell them that it indicates an approximate answer. Give students 10 to 15 seconds to determine which is the closest estimate.

Ask two or three students to explain which estimate they think is closest and why.

Students might say:

"840 is closest because 42 × 20 = 840."

"800 is closest because 42 × 20 = 840, but 20 is 2 groups of 42 larger, so 800 is closer."

We agree that 800 and 840 are both close estimates but that 800 is closest. Is 800 greater or less than the actual answer? How do you know? Figure it out by thinking about the numbers, and not finding the actual answer. Talk to a neighbor.

Ask students to explain their reasoning.

Students might say:

"800 is greater than the actual answer. If you use 42 × 20, that's 840. But that's 2 groups of 42 larger, and that's 84. 840 − 84 is going to be less than 800."

Repeat the procedure with Problem 2.

2. 67 × 45 ≈ 280 2,800 28,000

Students might say:

"It has to be 2,800. 280 would be the same as 70 × 4, and 28,000 would be 700 × 40."

"2,800 is going to be less than the actual answer. If you use 70 × 40 to get 2,800, that's a few more groups of 45, but it's also 5 groups of 67 less. So I think it is going to be bigger than 2,800."

This problem was a little different because you had to decide whether the answer was in the hundreds, thousands, or ten thousands. As you continue doing these *Closest Estimate* problems, some of them will be like this one—deciding how large the answer is. You'll also be doing *Closest Estimate* division problems.

If time remains, repeat the same procedure with Problem 3.

 ACTIVITY

25 MIN CLASS

2 Related Problems

This activity focuses on how adding and subtracting multiples of 10, 100, and 1,000 help students solve problems with large numbers.

We're going to continue working with large numbers today, including numbers over 10,000. We'll start by solving related problems. As I uncover each problem, think about how the answer to the previous problem can help you solve the new problem. You should be able to do these problems mentally.

Write these problems on the overhead (uncovering one at a time) or write them on the board, one at a time.

$$12{,}385 - 200 =$$
$$12{,}385 - 210 =$$
$$12{,}385 - 212 =$$

Ask for students' explanations for how they solved $12{,}385 - 200$ *(12,185)*. Then uncover the second problem. Give students a minute or two, and then ask for their solutions.

What is the answer to $12{,}385 - 210$? *(12,175)* How did you find the answer? Did anyone use the answer to $12{,}385 - 200$ to help solve this problem?

Uncover the third problem, give students a minute or two to think, and then ask the same kinds of questions about their solutions.

Visualizing the relationship among these three problems can be challenging. Ask students for a simple subtraction story context (or provide one yourself that is familiar to your students) and talk through the problem, using that context. Here is an example:

There are 12,385 people at a basketball game. If 200 of them leave the game, we know that 12,185 are left.

Use this story to tell me what $12{,}385 - 210$ means. Will the answer to this problem be more or less than 12,185? How do you know? What about the answer to $12{,}385 - 212$? How does that work with this story? Is the answer more or less than the answer to $12{,}385 - 210$?

Students might say:

"The first time, 200 people leave, but the second time, an extra 10 people leave. So there are fewer people left at the game by 10."

"If 212 people leave, it's like there are 212 empty seats. Before, there were only 200 empty seats. You subtracted more, so there aren't as many people left."

Ask students to reflect on the three problems.

When you first look at the third problem, does it look hard? Why or why not? Did solving the first two problems make it easier?

Listen for students' ideas about how the three problems relate to breaking up 212 by place and subtracting 200, then 10 more, and then another 2. Ask students to compare 12,385 with the result of each problem. Which digits are the same? Which are different? Why?

Present another set of related problems, one at a time.

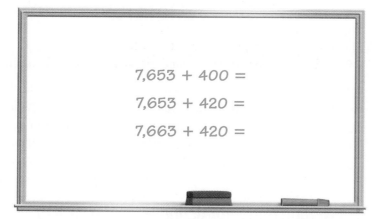

$$7,653 + 400 =$$
$$7,653 + 420 =$$
$$7,663 + 420 =$$

After students solve the first problem *(7,653 + 400 = 8,053)*, ask students to compare 7,653 and the sum 8,053. Which digits are the same? Which are different? Why?

Ask students to solve the second problem. Ask them to compare the sum of the first problem with the sum of the second problem. Then uncover the final problem. There may be some initial confusion until students realize that the first addend is the one that is different. Ask students to explain how they solved 7,663 + 420. *(8,083)* Did they use the answer to 7,653 + 420 and realize that the answer would be 10 more?

Ask students to apply a story context similar to the one you used for the first problem set. Then have them look at the final problem, and ask how the first two problems helped them solve the third.

Is there another easy way you could think of to add the two numbers in the last problem?

Some students may suggest using a calculator. Others may mention lining the numbers up and adding. Some may also say that you could add the 63 and the 20 together and get 83; combine the 7,600 and the

▲ **Student Activity Book, p. 13**

▲ **Student Activity Book, p. 14**

400 to make 8,000; and then combine the 83 and the 8,000 to get 8,083. Stress that, although the number looks big, it is fairly easy to solve mentally or in just a few steps.

These two problems, $12,385 − 212$ and $7,663 + 420$, might look difficult at first because the numbers are large. But you can see that if we look at the numbers and think about their relationships and about place value, the solutions are fairly easy. You'll work on more related problems like the ones we just did in the Math Workshop.

MATH WORKSHOP

3 **Adding and Subtracting Large Numbers**   25 MIN

Students continue focusing on place value and working with large numbers. Students should have time to work on three activities in this Math Workshop, which continues in the next session. You might want to have certain students work on Activity 3A rather than having them do one of the other activities. (See the notes for Activity 3A below.)

3A **Adding and Subtracting Multiples of 100**   GROUPS

Not all students will need to do this activity. Choose this activity to give you time to work with a small group of students on locating numbers on the 10,000 chart and adding and subtracting multiples of 100 and 1,000 on the chart. Also, students who did not complete *Student Activity Book* pages 2 and 3 in Session 1.2 may do so during this activity.

For a full description of this activity, see Session 1.2, pages 34–35.

3B **Related Problems**   INDIVIDUALS

On *Student Activity Book* pages 13–14, students solve related addition and subtraction problems involving 5-digit numbers as discussed on pages 45–47. There is not much space on these pages for students to show their work because they are expected to do these problems mentally. Note that in some of the problems, the first number changes, so students should look carefully at both numbers in each problem and think about the relationships among the problems in each set. They should also think carefully about the operations of addition and subtraction in solving these problems. For example, in addition, the sum is the same regardless of which addend changes. In subtraction, however, students need to think about which number changes and how that affects the difference.❷

ONGOING ASSESSMENT: Observing Students at Work

Students solve sets of related addition or subtraction problems.

- **Do students use their knowledge of adding and subtracting multiples of 10, 100, and 1,000 to solve the related addition or subtraction problems?**

- **Can students estimate about how much the sum or difference will be?**

- **Do students use their understanding of subtraction as they use one problem in a set to solve the next problem?** Do they know how the change in one number affects the answer? (For example, in Problem 2, they solve 8,000 − 30, which is 7,970. The next problem is 8,010 − 30. Do students realize that they need to add 10 to the previous answer? The next problem is 8,010 − 38. Do students realize that they need to subtract 8 more?)

As students are working, ask them questions about how they are using one problem in a set to solve the next problem. Encourage all students to solve these problems mentally.

DIFFERENTIATION: Supporting the Range of Learners

Intervention If a student is finding numbers in the thousands too difficult, alter the related problems to include numbers in the 100s and smaller numbers. Help students understand how a problem is related to the preceding one. Use story contexts or number lines to help students visualize the relationship. Ask questions such as the following:

- Are you subtracting more or less?

- How much more or less?

- Is your answer going to be larger or smaller?

- Is the starting number larger or smaller?

- How much larger or smaller?

- How will that affect your answer?

Algebra Note

❷ **Changing the Numbers in a Subtraction Problem** Using a related problem to solve a subtraction problem is more difficult for some students than using related problems to solve an addition problem. Consider Problem 3 on *Student Activity Book* page 13. 10,175 − 125 is easy to solve mentally. How does the difference, 10,050, help us solve 10,175 − 128? Is the answer 3 more or 3 less than 10,050? Students have studied the underlying ideas in Grade 4 and return to them in this unit. A story context or representation helps students visualize the relationship between these two subtraction expressions and keeps track of how changing one of the numbers changes the difference. Calling on a story context or a number line not only provides students with a tool for reasoning but also helps them form mental images of the operations and their properties. Students will discuss these ideas in Session 2.3. See more information in the section on equivalent problems in addition and subtraction in "Algebra Connections in This Unit," p. 16

Name _____ Date _____
Thousands of Miles, Thousands of Seats

More How Many Steps Problems

For each problem below, find out how many steps it is from the given number to 10,000 on the 10,000 chart. Use the 10,000 chart if it will help you. Show how you figured out your answer. For Problems 4 and 5, choose your own starting number.

1. Start at 852. How many steps to 10,000? _____

2. Start at 6,105. How many steps to 10,000? _____

3. Start at 7,001. How many steps to 10,000? _____

4. Start at _____. How many steps to 10,000? _____

5. Start at _____. How many steps to 10,000? _____

Sessions 1.4, 1.5   Unit 3   15

▲ **Student Activity Book, p. 15**

Teaching Note

❸ Practicing Division Facts In this unit, students review division facts and are assessed on them in Session 3.1, with the goal that all students become fluent with these division problems by the end of this unit.

Name _____ Date _____

Thousands of Miles, Thousands of Seats

Daily Practice

Division Practice 1

Solve each division problem below. Then write the related multiplication combination.

NOTE Students review division problems that are related to the multiplication combinations they know.

SMH 25–29, 38–39

Division Problem	Multiplication Combination
1. 63 ÷ 7 = _____	_____ × _____ = _____
2. 72 ÷ 9 = _____	_____ × _____ = _____
3. 56 ÷ 8 = _____ .	_____ × _____ = _____
4. 42 ÷ 6 = _____	_____ × _____ = _____
5. 121 ÷ 11 = _____	_____ × _____ = _____
6. 84 ÷ 7 = _____	_____ × _____ = _____
7. 48 ÷ 8 = _____	_____ × _____ = _____
8. 36 ÷ 9 = _____	_____ × _____ = _____
9. 7)42	_____ × _____ = _____
10. 9)54	_____ × _____ = _____

16 Unit 3   Session 1.4

▲ **Student Activity Book, p. 16**

Name _____ Date _____

Thousands of Miles, Thousands of Seats

Homework

More Related Problems

Solve these sets of problems. Think about how each problem in the set is related to the previous one.

NOTE Students solve sets of related problems. Encourage them to solve each problem mentally.

SMH 6, 8–9

1. 4,580 + 250 = _____ 4,580 + 253 = _____ 4,590 + 253 = _____	2. 7,800 − 50 = _____ 7,800 − 60 = _____ 7,800 − 70 = _____
3. 11,398 + 2,000 = _____ 11,398 + 2,100 = _____ 11,398 + 2,150 = _____	4. 24,356 + 400 = _____ 24,356 + 410 = _____ 24,356 + 419 = _____
5. 14,532 − 3,000 = _____ 14,532 − 2,999 = _____ 14,532 − 2,989 = _____	6. 55,436 − 20,000 = _____ 55,436 − 19,000 = _____ 55,436 − 19,100 = _____

Session 1.4   Unit 3 17

▲ **Student Activity Book, p. 17**

3C How Many Steps to 10,000?

INDIVIDUALS GROUPS

Students continue finding how far it is from the given number to 10,000. Each student completes *Student Activity Book* page 15 individually, but students will need to share the 10,000 charts. Help students choose numbers for Problems 4 and 5 that present a good level of challenge for them.

For a full description of this activity, see Session 1.3, pages 37–40.

3D Close to 1,000

PAIRS

Pairs play *Close to 1,000*. For a full description of this activity, see Session 1.3, pages 40–42.

SESSION FOLLOW-UP

4 Daily Practice and Homework

Daily Practice: For ongoing review, have students complete *Student Activity Book* page 16.❸

Homework: Students solve related addition and subtraction problems on *Student Activity Book* page 17.

Student Math Handbook: Students and families may use *Student Math Handbook* page G2 for reference and review. See pages 149–151 in the back of this unit.

Adding and Subtracting Large Numbers, *continued*

Math Focus Points

◆ Solving addition and subtraction problems with large numbers by focusing on the place value of the digits

◆ Reading, writing, and sequencing numbers to 10,000 and 100,000

◆ Learning the names of places larger than 100,000: million, billion, trillion

Vocabulary

million
billion
trillion

Today's Plan		Materials
MATH WORKSHOP **① Adding and Subtracting Large Numbers** **①A Adding and Subtracting Multiples of 100** **①B Related Problems** **①C How Many Steps to 10,000?** **①D *Close to 1,000***	🕐 **40 MIN**	**1A** • Materials from Session 1.2, p. 32 **1B** • *Student Activity Book,* pp. 13–14 (from Session 1.4) **1C** • Materials from Session 1.3, p. 36 • *Student Activity Book,* p. 15 (from Session 1.4) **1D** • Materials from Session 1.4, p. 43
DISCUSSION **② The Largest Number**	🕐 **20 MIN** 👥 **CLASS** 👥 **PAIRS**	• *Student Activity Book,* pp. 2–3 (optional)
SESSION FOLLOW-UP **③ Daily Practice**		• *Student Activity Book,* p. 19 • *Student Math Handbook,* pp. 6, 7; G2

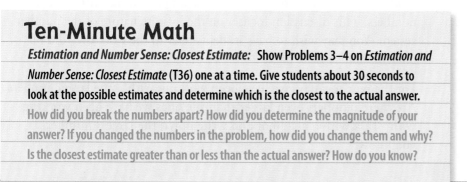

Ten-Minute Math

Estimation and Number Sense: Closest Estimate: Show Problems 3–4 on *Estimation and Number Sense: Closest Estimate* (T36) one at a time. Give students about 30 seconds to look at the possible estimates and determine which is the closest to the actual answer.

How did you break the numbers apart? How did you determine the magnitude of your answer? If you changed the numbers in the problem, how did you change them and why? Is the closest estimate greater than or less than the actual answer? How do you know?

① MATH WORKSHOP
Adding and Subtracting Large Numbers

40 MIN

The Math Workshop from Session 1.4 continues.

①A Adding and Subtracting Multiples of 100

GROUPS

Choose this activity for students who still need more time to complete *Student Activity Book* pages 2–3, or who need more practice locating numbers on the 10,000 chart and adding and subtracting multiples of 100 and 1,000 on the chart. These students work on this activity in place of one of the other activities.

①B Related Problems

INDIVIDUALS

For complete details, see Session 1.4, pages 48–49.

①C How Many Steps to 10,000?

INDIVIDUALS GROUPS

For complete details, see Session 1.3, pages 37–40 and Session 1.4, page 50.

①D Close to 1,000?

PAIRS

For complete details, see Session 1.3, pages 40–42.

② DISCUSSION
The Largest Number

20 MIN   CLASS   PAIRS

Math Focus Points for Discussion

◆ Learning the names of places larger than 100,000: million, billion, trillion

Students have spent time in this Investigation working with 5-digit numbers. This discussion focuses on the infinite nature of the number system. You may wish to have students refer to the work they did on *Student Activity Book* pages 2–3.

For the past few days we have been working with some large numbers. Are there numbers even larger than the ones we have been working with? Talk with a neighbor and write down the largest number you know.

Bring the class back together after a couple of minutes. Ask for students' comments. While some students may take a stab at writing a number with many digits, fifth graders are likely to know that "numbers go on forever." Ask students how they know.

Students might say:

"If you had enough things to count, you could just keep counting one more and one more. There is no end, except you might run out of things to count."

"You can always add one more."

Fifth graders are often very interested in the names of large numbers. Use this opportunity to see what names they know for numbers with more than 5 digits. Some students are likely to know million, billion, and trillion. Other students may have picked up the word *googol*, the number formed by the digit 1 followed by 100 zeros.

Work with students to say the names of large numbers.

1,000	one thousand
10,000	ten thousand
100,000	one hundred thousand
1,000,000	one million
1,000,000,000	one billion
1,000,000,000,000	one trillion

Then try some of the examples students wrote themselves or try a number in the millions that is not a multiple of 10. ❶

Teaching Note

❶ **Large Numbers** Students will continue to practice reading and writing large numbers in Ten-Minute Math activities in this unit and other units. They can also refer to the *Student Math Handbook*.

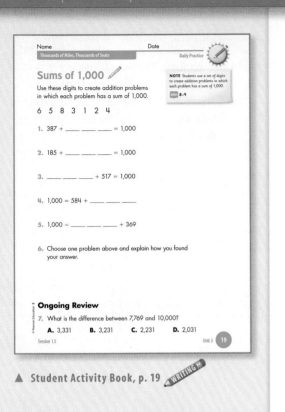

▲ Student Activity Book, p. 19

Now ask students to choose a really big number—something with more than 5 digits.

Write a really, really big number on your piece of paper.

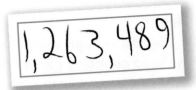

Add 10 to it and show how the new number is different. Add or subtract a few different numbers that are multiples of 10, 100, or 1,000 to your really big number and work with a partner to see how your number changes.

Allow students a chance to work with the large numbers they have created and see if students are making accurate changes as they add or subtract multiples of 10, 100, or 1,000.

SESSION FOLLOW-UP
3 Daily Practice

Daily Practice: For reinforcement of this unit's content, have students complete *Student Activity Book* page 19.

Student Math Handbook: Students and families may use *Student Math Handbook* pages 6, 7 and G2 for reference and review. See pages 149–151 in the back of this unit.

Mathematical Emphases

Computational Fluency Adding and subtracting accurately and efficiently

Math Focus Points

◆ Solving whole-number addition and subtraction problems efficiently

◆ Using clear and concise notation for recording addition and subtraction strategies

Whole-Number Operations Examining and using strategies for subtracting whole numbers

Math Focus Points

◆ Identifying, describing, and comparing subtraction strategies by focusing on how each strategy starts

◆ Analyzing and using different subtraction strategies

◆ Developing arguments about how the differences represented by two subtraction expressions are related (e.g., 1,208 − 297 and 1,208 − 300)

◆ Understanding the meaning of the steps and notation of the U.S. algorithm for subtraction

Studying Subtraction

	Student Activity Book	Student Math Handbook	Professional Development: Read Ahead of Time	
SESSION 2.1 p. 58				
Naming Subtraction Strategies Students solve a 3-digit subtraction problem and discuss their strategies. Strategies are classified and posted on chart paper to be used as a reference throughout the investigation.	20–23	10–13	• **Teacher Note:** Subtraction Strategies, p. 119 • **Teacher Note:** Describing, Comparing, and Classifying Subtraction Strategies, p. 123 • **Dialogue Box:** Classifying and Naming Subtraction Strategies, p. 145	
SESSION 2.2 p. 64				
Practicing Subtraction Students continue to practice solving subtraction problems and focus on clear notation. They are encouraged to try strategies that they may not normally use.	25–30	10–13		
SESSION 2.3 p. 69				
Subtraction Starter Problems Students solve subtraction problems in different ways by using given first steps. They discuss how changing a number in a subtraction problem (e.g., changing 1,208 − 297 to 1,208 − 300) affects the difference.	31–33	10–13	• **Teacher Note:** Reasoning and Proof in Mathematics, p. 125	
SESSION 2.4 p. 75				
Studying the U.S. Algorithm Students study the steps and notation for the U.S. algorithm for subtraction. They solve more subtraction problems in a Math Workshop, using strategies they have been studying in this investigation.	25, 34–42	13	• **Teacher Note:** Why Study the U.S. Conventional Algorithms?, p. 128 • **Dialogue Box:** Working with the U.S. Algorithm, p. 147	
SESSION 2.5 p. 81				
Assessment: Subtraction Problems Students continue the Math Workshop from Session 2.4, solving subtraction problems using strategies they have been studying in this investigation. Students are assessed on their ability to efficiently solve two subtraction problems.	25, 34–40, 43, 45–46	10–13	• **Teacher Note:** Assessment: Subtraction Problems, p. 131	

Ten-Minute Math See page 20 for an overview.

Practicing Place Value
- No materials needed

Estimation and Number Sense: Closest Estimate
- T36–T38, *Estimation and Number Sense: Closest Estimate* (pages 1–3 of 3) 🖥

Materials to Gather	Materials to Prepare
• Chart paper	
• T39, Map of the Continental United States 🖥	• **Chart paper** Write the title "Clear and Concise Notation" on a sheet of chart paper. (optional)
	• **M14, Map of the Continental United States** Make copies. (as needed)
• **M14, Map of the Continental United States** (as needed; from Session 2.4) • **Charts showing subtraction strategies** (from Session 2.1)	• **M15, Assessment: Subtraction Problems** Make copies. (1 per student)

🖥 Overhead Transparency

Naming Subtraction Strategies

Math Focus Points

- Solving whole-number addition and subtraction problems efficiently
- Identifying, describing, and comparing subtraction strategies by focusing on how each strategy starts

Vocabulary

subtracting in parts
adding up
subtracting back
changing the numbers to make an easier problem
subtracting by place

Today's Plan | Materials

1 ACTIVITY **Solving a Subtraction Problem**	10 MIN INDIVIDUALS	
2 DISCUSSION **Subtraction Strategies**	30 MIN CLASS	• Chart paper
3 ACTIVITY **Practicing Subtraction**	20 MIN INDIVIDUALS	• *Student Activity Book,* pp. 20–21
4 SESSION FOLLOW-UP **Daily Practice and Homework**		• *Student Activity Book,* pp. 22–23 • *Student Math Handbook,* pp. 10–13

Ten-Minute Math

Estimation and Number Sense: Closest Estimate Show Problems 4–6 on *Estimation and Number Sense: Closest Estimate* (T36) one at a time. Give students about 30 seconds to look at the possible estimates and determine which is the closest to the actual answer. Have two or three students explain their reasoning for each problem.

Ask students:

- How did you break the numbers apart?
- How did you determine the magnitude of your answer?
- If you changed the numbers in the problem, how did you change them and why?
- Is the closest estimate greater than or less than the actual answer? How do you know?

ACTIVITY
1 Solving a Subtraction Problem

10 MIN **INDIVIDUALS**

The work in this investigation is about examining and practicing strategies for subtraction.❶ It is expected that students will come into Grade 5 with a solid understanding of the operation of subtraction. They are also expected to have at least one strategy for subtracting 3-digit and 4-digit numbers that they use accurately and efficiently. In this investigation, students consolidate their previous work on the operation of subtraction as they work on the following:

- Articulating the mathematics of the strategies that they use

- Considering and trying out other strategies that may be new to them, including the U.S. algorithm

- Using clear and concise notation to show their strategies and solutions

Tell students that you know that last year they spent quite a bit of time working on subtraction. Explain that today the class is going to take a look at some of the strategies that students use to subtract and will practice solving subtraction problems.

Write the following subtraction problem on the board. Ask students to solve the problem and record their strategy on paper.❷

$$892 - 567 =$$

As you circulate and observe students working, see which strategies are being used and which are not being used. The discussion on page 60 is based on the first step students take in solving the problem. Look for examples of the following first steps for solving $892 - 567$:

Subtracting in parts

$$892 - 500 \qquad \text{or} \qquad 892 - 100$$

Adding up

(Using this strategy, students "add up" from 567 until they reach 892.)

$$567 + 3 \qquad \text{or} \qquad 567 + 100 \qquad \text{or} \qquad 567 + 33$$

Subtracting back

(Using this strategy, students "subtract back" until they reach 567.)

$$892 - 100 \qquad \text{or} \qquad 892 - 200$$

Professional Development
❶ **Teacher Note:** Subtraction Strategies, p. 119

Math Note
❷ **Using "Minus" Instead of "Take Away"** When reading subtraction problems aloud, say 892 *minus* 567 (instead of 892 *take away* 567). By using *minus* instead of *take away*, you are presenting the problem without implying that the solution will be found by "taking away" the smaller number from the larger. Because there are many kinds of situations for which subtraction is useful (i.e., removing some amount, comparing, and finding a missing part), it is important that students see the "−" sign as an indicator of any kind of subtraction situation.

Professional Development

❸ **Teacher Note:** Describing, Comparing, and Classifying Subtraction Strategies, p. 123

❹ **Dialogue Box:** Classifying and Naming Subtraction Strategies, p. 145

Math Note

❺ **Is the Number Line a Strategy?** Students used a number line to represent their strategies in Investigation 1 and may choose to continue to use it for these problems. Some students might say, "My strategy is to use a number line." If so, stress that the number line is not a strategy; it is a tool that makes a strategy more visible. It can represent a number of different strategies. In this discussion, a strategy is classified according to the kind of mathematical steps taken to solve the problem. However, students may like to add number lines to some of the charts to *illustrate* a strategy.

Teaching Note

❻ **The U.S. Algorithm** It is possible that some students in your class will be using the U.S. algorithm for subtraction. If it comes up, post this strategy on a chart titled "Subtracting by Place." Students study the notation of this algorithm in Session 2.4.

Changing the numbers to make an easier problem to solve

$$892 - 570 \qquad \text{or} \qquad 895 - 570$$

ONGOING ASSESSMENT: Observing Students at Work

Students solve a subtraction problem.

- **Do all students have at least one strategy for solving a subtraction problem?**

- **What strategies are students using?** Are they breaking numbers apart or changing one or both numbers?

- **How efficiently are students using strategies?** Can students add or subtract groups of 10? What are the largest numbers students are using as they add up, subtract back, or break a number into parts?

DISCUSSION
② Subtraction Strategies

30 MIN   CLASS

Math Focus Points for Discussion

◆ Identifying, describing, and comparing subtraction strategies by focusing on how each strategy starts

In this discussion, students explain their subtraction strategies.❸ ❹ ❺ These strategies are recorded on chart paper and grouped by the first step taken. These charts stay posted throughout the remainder of the unit.

Inform students that as they explain their solutions, you are going to write the different strategies on charts, grouping them by the first step students took when they solved the problem.❻ As students share, model a general mathematical description of each strategy. For instance, the first student may say that he started by solving $892 - 500$.

[Alex], I see that you subtracted a chunk of the second number.

Have the student explain the rest of his solution, and then ask this question:

Is there anyone else who started with 892 and subtracted part of 567?

Add that solution to the same chart. Explain to students the importance of naming strategies.

Having a name or phrase attached to each strategy will make it easier for us to refer to the strategies. Let's name the strategies by using a phrase to describe what is happening mathematically.

Have students agree on a short mathematical phrase that names each strategy, and write that at the top of the chart.

Students explain various subtraction strategies and choose a name for each one.

Ask students whether anyone used a different strategy (adding up, subtracting back, changing the numbers, and any other starts your students identify as being different), and follow the same procedure on a new chart.

Decide whether you want to introduce a start that no student has used. For example, if no one suggests changing one of the numbers, you may want to write it on the chart and ask students to think about it (e.g., 892 − 570 or 895 − 570).

ACTIVITY

20 MIN INDIVIDUALS

3 Practicing Subtraction

Students solve the subtraction problems on *Student Activity Book* pages 20–21. Tell students that as they solve the problems, they should think about the strategies they have talked about today. Use the names of the different strategies your students identified earlier in the session. They should use the strategies they normally use but should also try other strategies.

Name _____ Date _____
Thousands of Miles, Thousands of Seats

Subtraction Problems (page 1 of 2)

Solve each problem in two ways. Record your strategy for each solution.

1.   1,569 − 275 = _____

First way:	Second way:

2. There are 813 students in Talisha's school. Today, 768 are present. How many are absent?

First way:	Second way:

20 Unit 3   Session 2.1

▲ **Student Activity Book, p. 20**

Name _____ Date _____
Thousands of Miles, Thousands of Seats

Subtraction Problems (page 2 of 2)

3. Mitch had $10.13 in his wallet. On the way home from school he spent $5.79. How much money does he have left?

First way:	Second way:

4.   1,205
         − 625

First way:	Second way:

Session 2.1   Unit 3 21

▲ **Student Activity Book, p. 21**

ONGOING ASSESSMENT: Observing Students at Work

Students solve subtraction problems in two ways.

- **Do all students have at least one strategy for solving a subtraction problem?**

- **What strategies are students using?** Can students add or subtract multiples of 10 and 100? What are the largest numbers that students are adding up or subtracting? Do students create equivalent problems?

DIFFERENTIATION: Supporting the Range of Learners

Adjust numbers as needed for all students. If students are fluent with one strategy, encourage them to work for fluency with another strategy. The number line is a useful representation for all students as they develop fluency with strategies.

Intervention Some students may still be developing fluency with subtraction. Those students should solve the problem in only one way.

Extension If students need to be challenged, ask them to try creating equivalent problems that are easier to solve.

$$1,569 - 275 = \boxed{1,294}$$

$$1,569 - 200 = 1,369$$
$$1,369 - 60 = 1,309$$
$$1,309 - 5 = 1,304$$
$$1,304 - 10 = 1,294$$

Sample Student Work

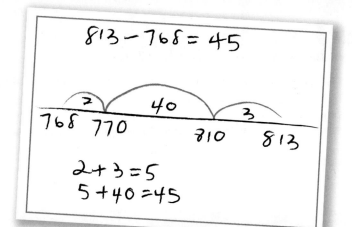

Sample Student Work

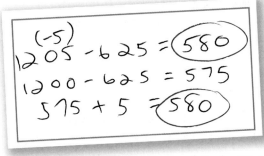

Sample Student Work

Division Practice 2

Solve each division problem below. Then write the related multiplication combination.

NOTE Students review division problems that are related to the multiplication combinations they know. Skill 25–29, 38–39

Division Problem	Multiplication Combination
1. $32 \div 4 =$ _____	_____ × _____ = _____
2. $72 \div 8 =$ _____	_____ × _____ = _____
3. $28 \div 7 =$ _____	_____ × _____ = _____
4. $42 \div 7 =$ _____	_____ × _____ = _____
5. $88 \div 11 =$ _____	_____ × _____ = _____
6. $84 \div 12 =$ _____	_____ × _____ = _____
7. $45 \div 5 =$ _____	_____ × _____ = _____
8. $81 \div 9 =$ _____	_____ × _____ = _____
9. $3\overline{)18}$	_____ × _____ = _____
10. $8\overline{)96}$	_____ × _____ = _____

Name _____ Date _____

Thousands of Miles, Thousands of Seats — *Daily Practice*

▲ **Student Activity Book, p. 22**

SESSION FOLLOW-UP

4 Daily Practice and Homework

Daily Practice: For ongoing review, have students complete *Student Activity Book* page 22.

Homework: Students solve subtraction problems involving 3-digit and 4-digit numbers on *Student Activity Book* page 23.

Student Math Handbook: Students and families may use *Student Math Handbook* pages 10–13 for reference and review. See pages 149–151 in the back of this unit.

Name _____ Date _____

Thousands of Miles, Thousands of Seats — *Homework*

Practicing Subtraction

Solve each subtraction problem and show your solutions.

NOTE Students practice solving subtraction problems presented in different ways. Skill 10–13

1. $734 - 566 =$ _____

2. $\begin{array}{r} 2,462 \\ -1,269 \\ \hline \end{array}$

3. Nora had $12.75. She spent $4.95 on baseball cards. How much money does she have left?

4. There are 524 students at Adams School. Today, 47 are absent. How many students are at school?

▲ **Student Activity Book, p. 23**

Practicing Subtraction

Math Focus Points

◆ Solving whole-number addition and subtraction problems efficiently

◆ Using clear and concise notation for recording addition and subtraction strategies

Today's Plan		Materials
① DISCUSSION **Notating Solutions**	20 MIN CLASS PAIRS	• Chart paper (optional)*
② ACTIVITY **Solving Distance Problems**	40 MIN INDIVIDUALS	• *Student Activity Book*, pp. 25–27 • T39
③ SESSION FOLLOW-UP **Daily Practice and Homework**		• *Student Activity Book*, pp. 28–30 • *Student Math Handbook*, pp. 10–13

*See *Materials to Prepare*, p. 57.

Ten-Minute Math

Estimation and Number Sense: Closest Estimate Show Problems 7–9 on *Estimation and Number Sense: Closest Estimate* (T37) one at a time. Give students about 30 seconds to look at the possible estimates and determine which is the closest to the actual answer. Have two or three students explain their reasoning for each problem. Ask students:

• How did you break the numbers apart?

• How did you determine the magnitude of your answer?

• If you changed the numbers in the problem, how did you change them and why?

• Is the closest estimate greater than or less than the actual answer?

• How do you know?

DISCUSSION

1 Notating Solutions

20 MIN   CLASS   PAIRS

Math Focus Points for Discussion

◆ Using clear and concise notation for recording addition and subtraction strategies

If you think your class might find it useful, briefly review each of the subtraction strategies your class posted yesterday.

Write the following problem on the board. Give students a few minutes to solve it and record each step carefully. Tell students that the focus of this discussion is on clear and concise notation and that they should write their solution as clearly as possible.

$$685 - 378 =$$

It is important to record your solutions clearly and concisely for two reasons. First, it helps you keep track of your work, and second, you can communicate your thinking in a way that others can easily understand.

Students trade papers with a partner and try to follow their partner's strategy. Give students a chance to discuss each other's strategies.

What makes a strategy hard to follow? What makes it easy? What makes the way you write down a strategy clear and concise?

Allow several students to offer their ideas. You may choose to create a chart titled "Clear and Concise Notation". Ideas that could be noted by you or the students may include the ones shown on the next page.

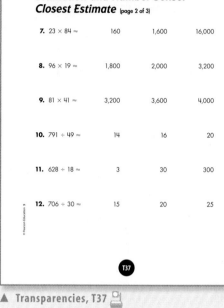

Thousands of Miles, Thousands of Seats			
Estimation and Number Sense: Closest Estimate (page 2 of 3)			
7. $23 \times 84 \approx$	160	1,600	16,000
8. $96 \times 19 \approx$	1,800	2,000	3,200
9. $81 \times 41 \approx$	3,200	3,600	4,000
10. $791 \div 49 \approx$	14	16	20
11. $628 \div 18 \approx$	3	30	300
12. $706 \div 30 \approx$	15	20	25

T37

▲ Transparencies, T37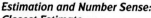

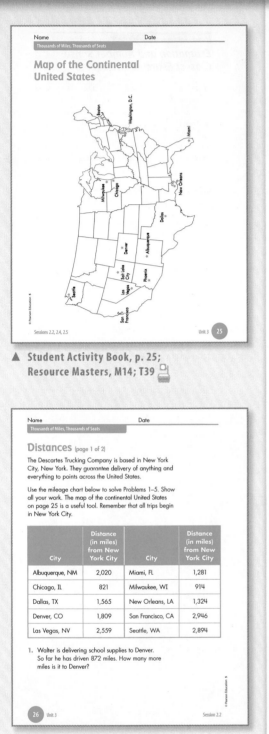

▲ Student Activity Book, p. 25;
Resource Masters, M14; T39

▲ Student Activity Book, p. 26

Clear and Concise Notation

Clear Notation

Steps are written in a sequence that is easy to follow. They are not all over the page.

If you look at the solution a week from now, you will still know how you solved the problem.

Concise Notation

Steps are combined when possible. Larger jumps are easier to follow.

Example: $685 - 300 = 385$ is more concise than:

$685 - 100 = 585$
$585 - 100 = 485$
$485 - 100 = 385$

Enough steps are included that the strategy can be understood. Not every single step, especially those done mentally, needs to be included.

Example: $685 - 378 = $ _____

First step: $685 - 380$ It is obvious that 2 was added to the 378.

Students may also be able to give good examples of what helps them keep their notation clear. Keep this conversation focused on positive examples rather than negative ones. Remind students that there is not one best way to record strategies. Also remind them that finding notation that is clear and concise to others is an important piece of mathematics and will be very useful in a variety of situations.

ACTIVITY

2 Solving Distance Problems

40 MIN INDIVIDUALS

Place the transparency of the Map of the Continental United States (T39) on the overhead and have students also refer to the map on *Student Activity Book* page 25. Have a brief discussion about what the map shows and whether students have ever visited any of the specified cities. You may also ask them to share memories of trips they have taken (e.g., how far they went, how long it took to get there, wondering how much farther they had to go, and so on).

A student shares prior knowledge about various cities in the United States in preparation for solving subtraction problems involving distances.

Students spend the rest of the session solving subtraction problems on *Student Activity Book* pages 26–27. All of the problems involve the distance of different U.S. cities from New York City. As students work, ask them to focus on these two important goals:

• Trying different strategies from the subtraction charts

• Making sure that their notation is clear and concise

Also remind students that the number line may be a useful tool for them to use as they solve these problems.

Circulate as students work, asking them to explain their strategies clearly and encouraging students to try out different strategies.

✔ ONGOING ASSESSMENT: Observing Students at Work

Students solve subtraction problems.

• **What strategies are students using to solve problems?** Are most students mainly using one strategy? Are a variety of strategies being used?

• **Are students efficiently using strategies?** Are they taking the largest chunk of numbers possible (e.g., 400 instead of 100, 100, 100, 100)?

• **Are students clearly notating their work?** Is the work clear enough that anyone looking at it could understand their thinking?

Name _____ Date _____

Thousands of Miles, Thousands of Seats

Distances (page 2 of 2)

2. Rachel is driving a trailer of new cars to Dallas. She is 480 miles from Dallas. How many miles has she driven so far?

3. On her next trip, Rachel drives a moving truck to San Francisco. She has driven 1,389 miles. How many more miles is it to San Francisco?

4. Walter is delivering a truck full of canned goods to New Orleans. On the first day he drives 489 miles, and on the second day he drives 616 miles. How many miles is he from New Orleans?

5. On their next trips, Rachel drives to Seattle and Walter drives to Milwaukee. How many more miles does Rachel drive than Walter?

Session 2.2   Unit 3   27

▲ **Student Activity Book, p. 27**

Name _____ Date _____

Thousands of Miles, Thousands of Seats   Daily Practice

Solving Division Problems

NOTE Students practice solving division problems.
SMH 38–39

1. **a.** Write a story problem that represents 704 ÷ 22.

   b. Solve 704 ÷ 22. Show your solution clearly.

2. **a.** Write a story problem that represents 18)‾450.

   b. Solve 18)‾450.

Ongoing Review

3. Which number is a multiple of 24?

   A. 58   **B.** 76   **C.** 84   **D.** 96

28   Unit 3   Session 2.2

▲ **Student Activity Book, p. 28** WRITING

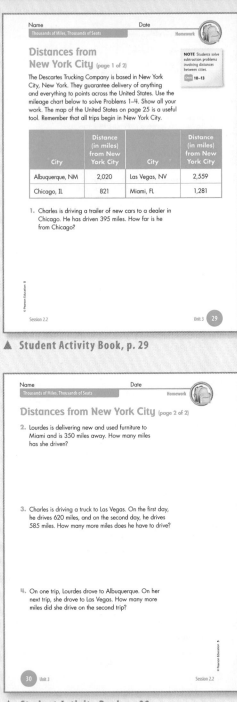

▲ **Student Activity Book, p. 29**

▲ **Student Activity Book, p. 30**

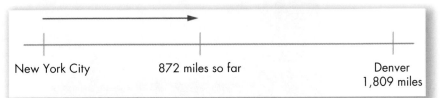

DIFFERENTIATION: Supporting the Range of Learners

Intervention For students still solidifying one subtraction strategy, ask them to explain each step to you, particularly how they start. Use the story context in the problem and a number line to help students visualize how to solve the problem. For example, a number line for Problem 1 might look like this:

New York City   872 miles so far   Denver
1,809 miles

Also ask students what they know about the relationships of the numbers and whether they are using as large a chunk (e.g., multiple groups of 10 or 100) as possible.

Extension If students are efficiently using one strategy, encourage them to try one of the other charted strategies.

All students should be encouraged to use the number line or story contexts to help them make sense of strategies.

SESSION FOLLOW-UP

③ Daily Practice and Homework

Daily Practice: For ongoing review, have students complete *Student Activity Book* page 28.

Homework: Students complete more subtraction problems involving distances on *Student Activity Book* pages 29–30.

Student Math Handbook: Students and families may use *Student Math Handbook* pages 10–13 for reference and review. See pages 149–151 in the back of this unit.

Subtraction Starter Problems

Math Focus Points

◆ Identifying, describing, and comparing subtraction strategies by focusing on how each strategy starts

◆ Analyzing and using different subtraction strategies

◆ Developing arguments about how the differences represented by two subtraction expressions are related (e.g., 1,208 − 297 and 1,208 − 300)

Today's Plan		Materials
ACTIVITY ❶ **Introducing Starter Problems**	15 MIN CLASS PAIRS	• *Student Activity Book*, pp. 31–32
ACTIVITY ❷ **Starter Problems**	30 MIN INDIVIDUALS	• *Student Activity Book*, pp. 31–32
DISCUSSION ❸ **Do I Add or Subtract?**	15 MIN CLASS PAIRS	
SESSION FOLLOW-UP ❹ **Daily Practice**		• *Student Activity Book*, p. 33 • *Student Math Handbook*, pp. 10–13

Ten-Minute Math

Estimation and Number Sense: Closest Estimate Show Problems 10–12 on *Estimation and Number Sense: Closest Estimate* (T37) one at a time. Give students about 30 seconds to look at the possible estimates and determine which is the closest to the actual answer. Have two or three students explain their reasoning for each problem. Ask students:

- How did you break the numbers apart?
- How did you determine the magnitude of your answer?
- If you changed the numbers in the problem, how did you change them and why?
- Is the closest estimate greater than or less than the actual answer?
- How do you know?

Teaching Note

❶ Individualizing Starter Problems The starter problems on *Student Activity Book* pages 31–32 for this session and pages 37–38 for Sessions 2.4 and 2.5 include these three starts:

• Subtracting in parts

• Adding up

• Changing the numbers

Perhaps your class has been using a different strategy, such as making an equivalent problem, or a place-value strategy using positive and negative numbers. If this is the case, and you want students to continue practicing this strategy, they can add that start to the problems. Students should also understand that they can change the start if that is not what they would use. For example, in Problem 1 on page 31 (2,168 − 455), the first start is 2,168 − 400. If students would subtract 100 first, they can write 2,168 − 100 as their start.

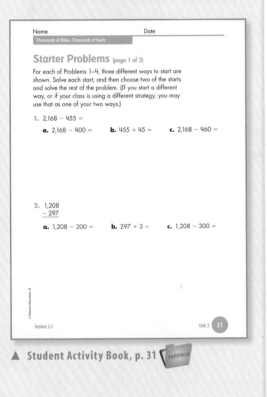

▲ Student Activity Book, p. 31

15 MIN   CLASS   PAIRS

① Introducing Starter Problems

You may want to briefly review the different strategies that students have been using and highlight new strategies that students have been trying.❶ Then ask all students to solve this problem:

$$1,423 - 776 =$$

Call on a student to share his or her first step and record it on the board. If possible, highlight the different starts that are used on *Student Activity Book* pages 31–32 (subtracting in parts, adding up, and changing the numbers). This is also a time to remind students that number lines and story contexts are helpful tools in solving subtraction problems.

Students might say:

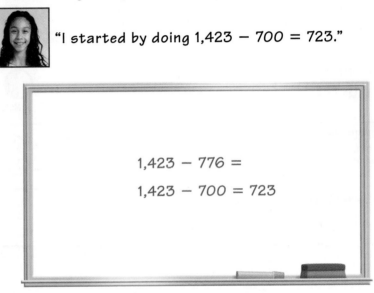

"I started by doing 1,423 − 700 = 723."

$$1,423 - 776 =$$
$$1,423 - 700 = 723$$

Before we solve the rest of the problem, let's think of a story context that will help us keep track of our solution. Who has a suggestion?

Students might suggest the travel context from yesterday's problems or another familiar context.

"Aunt Liz is driving 1,423 miles. If she's already gone 776 miles, how far does she still have to drive?"

When [Talisha] starts with 1,423 − 700 = 723, what part of the problem about Aunt Liz has she already solved? What does 700 mean? What does 723 represent? *(When Aunt Liz has gone 700 miles, she has 723 miles left to go.)*

What could [Talisha] do next to finish solving the problem? Talk to a neighbor and solve the rest of the problem, using [Talisha's] first step.

Ask students to share how they solved the rest of the problem and to explain their steps by using the story context.

Show one or two more examples of first steps your students used, following a similar format. If you do not have time to work with some of the first steps used by your students, acknowledge that there are other ways to start as well.

$$1,423 - 776 =$$
$$1,423 - 700 = 723$$
$$776 + 24 = 800$$
$$1,423 - 800 = 623$$

Today you are going to be given the first step of a problem. Your job is to complete the solution by starting with that first step.

ACTIVITY

② Starter Problems

30 MIN INDIVIDUALS

Students complete *Student Activity Book* pages 31–32. For each problem, students pick two of the three different starts and solve the problem. If the way students would start solving the problem is not included, they may include that as one of the ways to solve the problem, but then they should also choose one of the starts shown as their second way.❷ Make sure that all students complete Problem 2 before the discussion at the end of the session.

As students are working, circulate and make sure that they understand the task. Remind them that using the number line or a story context might be helpful. Ask them to explain each step of their solution and what they still have to figure out.

Name _____ Date _____
Thousands of Miles, Thousands of Seats

Starter Problems (page 2 of 2)

3. 6,563
   −1,418

   a. 6,563 − 1,400 =   **b.** 1,418 + 82 =   **c.** 6,563 − 1,500 =

4. 9,711 − 3,825 =
   a. 9,711 − 3,000 =   **b.** 3,825 + 75 =   **c.** 9,711 − 4,000 =

32 Unit 3   Session 2.3

▲ **Student Activity Book, p. 32**

Algebra Note

❷ **Why Try Different Strategies?** Students should be able to accurately and efficiently carry out one general strategy that works with any subtraction problem, such as subtracting in parts. However, after students are confident and competent in carrying out one strategy, they should try different strategies for two reasons. The first is that if students become comfortable with more than one strategy, they will have greater flexibility in choosing how to solve a particular problem. The second, and possibly more important, reason is that investigating how and why other strategies work helps students deepen their understanding of the operation. For example, using 1,208 − 300 to solve 1,208 − 297 in Problem 2 requires students to think through how increasing 297 by 3 affects the difference. By visualizing the relationship between 1,208 − 297 and 1,208 − 300 in a story context or on a number line, they think through the underlying mathematical properties of subtraction—properties that in later years can be expressed with algebraic notation.

ONGOING ASSESSMENT: Observing Students at Work

Students solve subtraction problems in two different ways.

- **Are students able to complete subtraction solutions by using two different starts?** If not, which strategies are they unable to use?

- **Are students using clear and concise notation to record their solutions?**

DIFFERENTIATION: Supporting the Range of Learners

Intervention Students who are still solidifying the use of one subtraction strategy to solve problems efficiently and accurately should solve each problem by using only that strategy. If some students have one subtraction strategy they can carry out well, but are reluctant to try a different strategy, encourage them to consider other strategies. Help them talk through a different approach, such as the following, using a subtraction story context that is familiar to the student:

You're really good at using the strategy of breaking apart the second number by place and subtracting the parts. I know that you can carry out this strategy very well, so I'm going to challenge you to think through a different first step for Problem 2. I know that you can easily subtract 300 from 1,208 mentally, so try the third first step (Part c). The tricky part is figuring out what to do next. Let's think of a story context to help with this. If there were 1,208 people at a movie and 300 of them left, 908 people would be left watching the movie. What if only 297 people left? Would there be more people than 908 left or fewer people left? How can 908 help you figure out the number left then?

15 MIN   CLASS   PAIRS

DISCUSSION

3 Do I Add or Subtract?

Math Focus Points for Discussion

◆ Developing arguments about how the differences represented by two subtraction expressions are related (e.g., $1,208 - 297$ and $1,208 - 300$)

This discussion focuses on what happens when you change one of the numbers in a subtraction problem to create an easier problem and then adjust the difference. This idea was explored more fully in Grade 4, and this discussion is intended to be a brief review. If you find that your students are struggling with this idea, plan on spending more time on it during the Math Workshop in the next two sessions.❸

On the board, write Problem 2 and the third starter.

1,208   1,208 − 300 = 908
− 297

How can you use 908, the difference between 1,208 and 300, to solve 1,208 − 297? What happens to the 3 that was added on to 297? With a partner, solve this problem by using the start on the board, or discuss it if you have already solved it. Be ready to explain how you knew whether you should add or subtract 3 from 908. Use a representation such as a drawing or a number line, or think of a story that will prove you are right to the class or to someone who comes to visit our class.❹

Give students a few minutes to solve this problem and then ask which pair is willing to explain their thinking.

Students might say:

 "We used a number line to show what's going on."

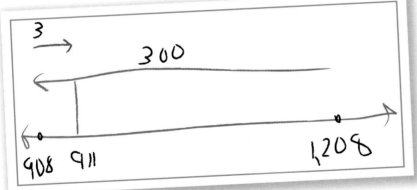

Sample Student Work

"We drew 12 hundreds and 8 ones. We crossed out 3 hundreds, but that was too much. So we put back 3 ones."

Professional Development

❸ **Teacher Note:** Reasoning and Proof in Mathematics, p. 125

Algebra Note

❹ **Using Images and Representations** Calling on a visual image such as a number line or developing a story context as a means to represent the situation provides students with tools for reasoning through such subtraction strategies and helps them understand how the operation of subtraction differs from that of addition. These representations help students keep track of the steps in the computation. They also help students form mental images of the operations and their properties. For more information, see "Algebra Connections in This Unit" on page 16.

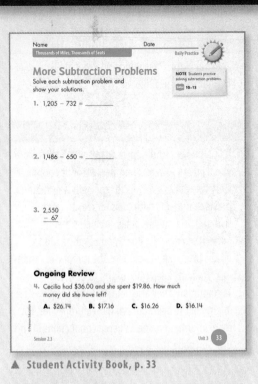

▲ Student Activity Book, p. 33

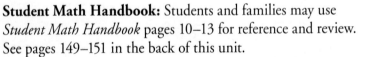

Sample Student Work

"We made up a story. I had $1,208 and owed Deon $297. I gave Deon $300 and was left with $908. I gave away too much, so Deon gave me back $3, and now I have $911."

SESSION FOLLOW-UP

4 Daily Practice

Daily Practice: For reinforcement of this unit's content, have students complete *Student Activity Book* page 33.

Student Math Handbook: Students and families may use *Student Math Handbook* pages 10–13 for reference and review. See pages 149–151 in the back of this unit.

Studying the U.S. Algorithm

Math Focus Points

◆ Understanding the meaning of the steps and notation of the U.S. algorithm for subtraction

◆ Solving whole-number addition and subtraction problems efficiently

◆ Analyzing and using different subtraction strategies

Vocabulary

algorithm

Today's Plan		Materials
① **ACTIVITY** **Examining the U.S. Algorithm**	30 MIN CLASS PAIRS	
② **MATH WORKSHOP** **Using Subtraction Strategies** **2A** The U.S. Algorithm **2B** More Starter Problems **2C** More Distance Problems	30 MIN	**2A** • *Student Activity Book,* pp. 34–36 **2B** • *Student Activity Book,* pp. 37–38 **2C** • *Student Activity Book,* p. 25 (from Session 2.2); pp. 39–40 • M14 (as needed)*
③ **SESSION FOLLOW-UP** **Daily Practice and Homework**		• *Student Activity Book,* pp. 41–42 • *Student Math Handbook,* p. 13

*See *Materials to Prepare,* p. 57.

Ten-Minute Math

Practicing Place Value Write on the board 2,180 = 2 thousands + 1 hundred + 8 tens + 0 ones. Ask students to fill in the blanks in the following sums for 2,180 and explain how they figured it out: 20 hundreds + _____ tens; 15 hundreds + _____ tens; _____ hundreds + 28 tens. Write on the board 4,028 = 4 thousands + 2 tens + 8 ones. Ask students to write 5 different combinations of thousands, hundreds, tens, and ones that equal 4,028. (For example: 2 thousands, 20 hundreds, 1 ten, and 18 ones; 3 thousands, 9 hundreds, 10 tens, and 28 ones)

Professional Development

❶ Teacher Note: Why Study the U.S. Conventional Algorithms?, p. 128

❷ Dialogue Box: Working with the U.S. Algorithm, p. 147

Math Notes

❸ The U.S. Algorithm The U. S. algorithm for subtraction, sometimes called "borrowing" or regrouping, is a procedure that was devised for compactness and efficiency. One advantage of the algorithm is that it requires only subtraction of single digits from numbers less than 20. However, its efficiency of steps and notation obscures the place value of the numbers. By examining the expanded notation of the numbers (e.g., 400 + 60 + 3) and the equivalent notation that results from regrouping the numbers (e.g., 400 + 50 + 13), students study the meaning of the algorithm. As with other strategies, studying this one and thinking through why these steps make sense allows students to deepen their knowledge about the operation of subtraction. Students who have developed good, efficient subtraction methods that they understand and can carry out easily, (such as subtracting in parts, adding up, or subtracting back,) may also benefit from practicing and becoming fluent in the U.S. algorithm. However, students are not expected to switch to using this algorithm. Continuing to use the methods they have developed will serve them well for their computation needs now and as adults.

❹ Using Positive Numbers Only A student may say (or you may choose to bring up) that you can subtract 8 from 4 and get −4 (negative four). Acknowledge that this is correct but that the U.S. algorithm for subtraction uses only positive numbers.

ACTIVITY

① Examining the U.S. Algorithm

30 MIN CLASS PAIRS

Tell students that today they are going to examine a subtraction strategy and notation that a number of people use—the U.S. algorithm for subtraction.❶ ❷ ❸

Write this problem on the board:

$$674$$
$$- \ 328$$

In this strategy, each place is subtracted separately. The people who invented this algorithm wanted to use only positive numbers. They figured out a way to rewrite the top number so that they could subtract each place and get all positive numbers. Let's look at how we could rewrite the top number to solve this problem.

When people use this U.S. algorithm, they start from the ones place. To help us understand this strategy better, first let's break the numbers apart by place.

Ask students how to break the numbers apart by place, and write the following on the board:

$$674 \qquad 600 + 70 + 4$$
$$- \ 328 \qquad - \ (300 + 20 + 8)$$

I wrote the bottom number in parentheses to show that we are subtracting *all* the parts. We start with the ones place, but we don't want to subtract 8 from 4. We want to change the way we're breaking up the number so that we get only positive differences.❹ We're going to break up the 70 and combine part of it with the 4.❺

Write 600 + 60 + _____ on the board next to the other problems, and ask students what number goes in the blank to still have a sum of 674.

Give students a moment to discuss this, and call on students to explain their thinking. Write 14 in the blank. Rewrite the rest of the problem. Then ask students what 14 − 8 is and write 6 under 14 − 8.

This is what is sometimes called "borrowing" or regrouping. We didn't have enough ones to subtract from, so we used one of the 7 tens and added it to 4. Then instead of 600 + 70 + 4, we had 600 + 60 + 14, which is still the same amount that is just broken up differently.

Ask students to subtract the 10s and then the 100s and record the results:

$$\begin{array}{r} 600 + 60 + 14 \\ - (300 + 20 + 8) \\ \hline 300 + 40 + 6 \end{array}$$

If needed, spend a few more minutes talking through how breaking up 674 in a new way allowed subtraction by place with a positive result in each place. If students seem to follow this easily, move on to examining the standard notation for this algorithm.

When people use this algorithm, they start with the ones place and use a shorthand notation instead of writing out the new way to break the number apart like we did. Let's look at the notation.

$$\begin{array}{cccc}
674 & 600 + 70 + 4 & 600 + 60 + 14 & \overset{6\ \ 1}{6\cancel{7}4} \\
- 328 & - (300 + 20 + 8) & - (300 + 20 + 8) & - 328 \\
& & \overline{300 + 40 + 6 = 346} & \overline{346}
\end{array}$$

As you write the algorithm on the board, talk through the procedure.

I don't want to subtract 8 from 4, so I take a ten from the tens place and give it to the ones place. I show this by crossing out the 7, making it a 6, and writing a 1 next to the 4 to make it 14. 14 − 8 is 6. Then 6 minus 2 is 4; that's 6 tens minus 2 tens. Then 6 minus 3 is 3. What do the 6 and the 3 mean?

Spend a few more minutes talking through this notation. Then work through another example in which both the 10s and 100s places must be changed.

$$\begin{array}{cccc}
463 & 400 + 60 + 3 & 400 + 50 + 13 & 300 + 150 + 13 \\
- 279 & - (200 + 70 + 9) & - (200 + 70 + 9) & - (200 + 70 + 9) \\
\hline & & & \overline{100 + 80 + 4 = 184}
\end{array}$$

Give students a few minutes to discuss these steps, and then talk through the shorthand notation. Let students know that if this algorithm still

Math Note

⑤ **Algorithms** An algorithm is a step-by-step procedure that can be completely specified. The traditional U.S. algorithm is one such procedure. Some of the other strategies that students use are also algorithms, such as adding by place and subtracting by place. In using these strategies, exactly the same steps are followed for any problem. Other strategies, such as adding up to solve a subtraction problem, are not necessarily algorithms because students may choose different ways to add up. However, some versions of these strategies are, in fact, algorithmic.

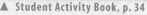

▲ **Student Activity Book, p. 34**

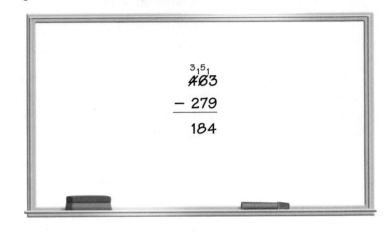

seems confusing, they will have time to think through this strategy during the Math Workshops today and tomorrow.

The U.S. Algorithm (page 2 of 3)

For Problems 3 and 4, use the U.S. algorithm to solve each problem. Also write the correct numbers in the blanks, showing how you broke apart the original numbers.

3.
```
  498        400  +  90  +  8
 -279       -(200  +  70  +  9)
```

```
  498       ____ + ____ + ____
 -279      -(____ + ____ + ____)
            ____ + ____ + ____
```

4.
```
  523        500  +  20  +  3
 -292       -(200  +  90  +  2)
```

```
  523       ____ + ____ + ____
 -292      -(____ + ____ + ____)
            ____ + ____ + ____
```

Sessions 2.4, 2.5   Unit 3   35

▲ Student Activity Book, p. 35

The U.S. Algorithm (page 3 of 3)

For Problem 5, use the U.S. algorithm to solve the problem. Also write the correct numbers in the blanks, showing how you broke apart the original numbers.

5.
```
  720        700  +  20  +  0
 -499       -(400  +  90  +  9)
```

```
  720       ____ + ____ + ____
 -499      -(____ + ____ + ____)
            ____ + ____ + ____
```

36   Unit 3   Sessions 2.4, 2.5

▲ Student Activity Book, p. 36

MATH WORKSHOP

30 MIN

2 Using Subtraction Strategies

This workshop provides you with time to work with individuals or small groups of students, helping them solidify strategies. Students should spend most of their time on starter problems (Activity 2B) and on the distance problems (Activity 2C). Continue emphasizing clear and concise notation.

. . . .

2A The U.S. Algorithm

INDIVIDUALS

On *Student Activity Book* pages 34–36, students practice breaking apart numbers to show how the U.S. algorithm for subtraction works.

ONGOING ASSESSMENT: Observing Students at Work

Students break apart numbers to show the steps of the U.S. algorithm for subtraction.

- **Do students understand how the numbers are broken apart to show regrouping?**

- **Can students use this algorithm to solve subtraction problems?**

DIFFERENTIATION: Supporting the Range of Learners

For students who have been using (or trying to use) this algorithm, these problems should provide support in helping them understand the mathematics of "borrowing."

Intervention For students who are still developing number and operation sense, this sheet will probably be confusing. These students may benefit from finding different ways to break apart the number. For example, 863 can be broken apart as $800 + 60 + 3$, or $800 + 50 + 13$, or $700 + 160 + 3$, and so on.

Extension Students who can explain and use the U.S. algorithm for the problems on this page can be challenged to solve problems that include zeros in the first number (e.g., $903 - 264$).

Some students may be ready to use the U.S. algorithm to solve subtraction problems with zeros in the first number.

2B More Starter Problems

INDIVIDUALS

On *Student Activity Book* pages 37–38, students solve subtraction problems in at least two ways, using two different starts. Encourage students to try strategies other than the one they normally use.

Problems 1 and 4 provide different opportunities for students to change numbers. Be aware of this, and decide whether you want to hold small group discussions. The third start for Problem 1 changes both numbers, and in Problem 4, the third start changes the first number.

For a full description of this activity, see Session 2.3, pages 70–72.

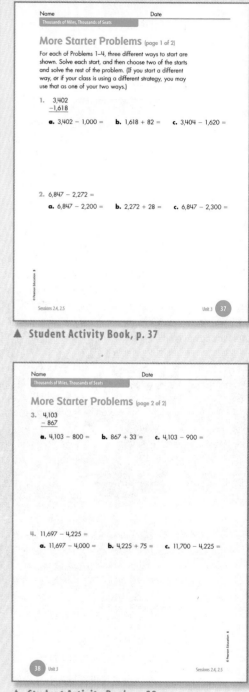

▲ Student Activity Book, p. 37

▲ Student Activity Book, p. 38

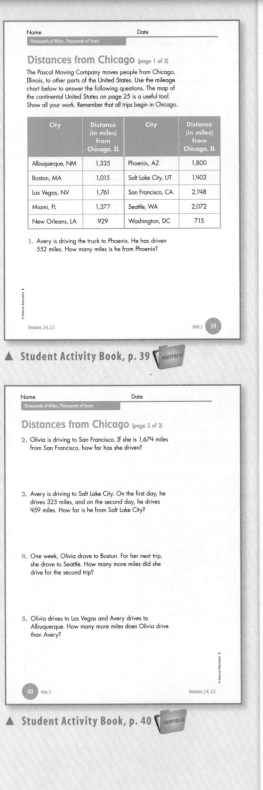

▲ **Student Activity Book, p. 39**

▲ **Student Activity Book, p. 40**

INDIVIDUALS

2C More Distance Problems

On *Student Activity Book* pages 39–40, students solve more distance problems. All trips begin in Chicago, Illinois. The map of the continental United States on *Student Activity Book* page 25 is a useful tool. Use the Map of the Continental United States (M14) to make more copies if necessary.

For a full description of this activity, see Session 2.2, pages 66–68.

SESSION FOLLOW-UP

3 Daily Practice and Homework

Daily Practice: For ongoing review, have students complete *Student Activity Book* page 41.

Homework: Students continue solving subtraction problems on *Student Activity Book* page 42.

Student Math Handbook: Students and families may use *Student Math Handbook* page 13 for reference and review. See pages 149–151 in the back of this unit.

Name _____ Date _____
Thousands of Miles, Thousands of Seats   Daily Practice

Division Practice 3

Solve each division problem below. Then write the related multiplication combination.

NOTE Students review division problems that are related to the multiplication combinations they know.
Skill 25–29

Division Problem	Multiplication Combination
1. 144 ÷ 12 = _____	_____ × _____ = _____
2. 32 ÷ 8 = _____	_____ × _____ = _____
3. 28 ÷ 4 = _____	_____ × _____ = _____
4. 56 ÷ 7 = _____	_____ × _____ = _____
5. 110 ÷ 11 = _____	_____ × _____ = _____
6. 64 ÷ 8 = _____	_____ × _____ = _____
7. 63 ÷ 9 = _____	_____ × _____ = _____
8. 27 ÷ 3 = _____	_____ × _____ = _____
9. 7)49	_____ × _____ = _____
10. 9)81	_____ × _____ = _____

Ongoing Review

11. Which number is **not** on the multiple tower for 18?

   A. 54   **B.** 108   **C.** 180   **D.** 192

Session 2.4   Unit 3   41

▲ **Student Activity Book, p. 41**

Name _____ Date _____
Thousands of Miles, Thousands of Seats   Homework

Subtraction Practice

Solve each subtraction problem and show your solutions.

NOTE Students have been practicing different ways to solve subtraction problems and writing their solutions using clear and concise notation.
Skill 10–13

1. 4,835 − 2,540 = _____

2. Tavon has 773 baseball cards in his collection. Janet has 1,215 in hers. How many more cards does Tavon need to collect in order to have the same number as Janet?

3. 6,789
   − 2,199

4. 2,205 − 1,789 = _____

42   Unit 3   Session 2.4

▲ **Student Activity Book, p. 42**

Assessment: Subtraction Problems

Math Focus Points

◆ Solving whole-number addition and subtraction problems efficiently

Today's Plan		Materials
① DISCUSSION **Using Strategies** 🕐 👫 15 MIN CLASS		• Charts showing subtraction strategies (from Session 2.1)
② ASSESSMENT ACTIVITY **Subtraction Problems** ✔ 🕐 👤 15 MIN INDIVIDUALS		• M15*
③ MATH WORKSHOP **Using Subtraction Strategies** 🕐 30 MIN **③A** The U.S. Algorithm **③B** More Starter Problems **③C** More Distance Problems		**③A** • *Student Activity Book,* pp. 34–36 (from Session 2.4) **③B** • *Student Activity Book,* pp. 37–38 (from Session 2.4) **③C** • *Student Activity Book,* p. 25 (from Session 2.2); pp. 39–40 (from Session 2.4) • M14 (as needed)
④ SESSION FOLLOW-UP **Daily Practice and Homework**		• *Student Activity Book,* pp. 43, 45–46 • *Student Math Handbook,* pp. 10–13

*See *Materials to Prepare,* p. 57.

Ten-Minute Math

Practicing Place Value   Write on the board 9,765 = 9 thousands +
7 hundreds + 6 tens + 5 ones. Ask students to fill in the blanks in the following
sums: _____ hundreds + 65 ones; _____ thousands + 17 hundreds + 65.
Write on the board 6,405 = 6 thousands + 4 hundreds + 5 ones. Ask students
to write 5 other combinations of place values for 6,405.

DISCUSSION

1 Using Strategies

15 MIN   CLASS

Math Focus Points for Discussion

◆ Solving whole-number addition and subtraction problems efficiently

This discussion can occur at either the beginning or the end of this session. If you think that students need more time solving subtraction problems before engaging in this discussion, save the last 15 minutes of class for it.

Make sure that the charts of subtraction strategies are posted for reference throughout this session.

We have several subtraction strategies listed on these charts and have spent a few days studying and practicing subtraction strategies. Is there one strategy that you feel the most confident with? Are they all equally easy to use? Is there one that you tend to use often? One that you don't use very much at all?

Have several students share their thoughts about this. This is an opportunity for students to review all the strategies and consider how they usually solve problems. It is also useful for you to hear how confident students are about these strategies.

Although it is not expected that all students become fluent with all of these strategies, it is important for all students to understand how each strategy works.

Write the following problems on the board:

$$6,415 - 5,198 = \qquad 4,824 - 2,539 =$$

Look at these two problems. Would you solve them the same way? Why or why not? Are there certain strategies that you use when you solve certain problems?

Ask students to consider this. The purpose of this discussion is to encourage students to look carefully at the numbers in the problems as they decide what subtraction strategy to use. There is no "right" answer to this question.

Students might say:

"I get the different strategies, but I know I can always solve the problem by adding up. So I'd solve both these problems the same way."

"I usually subtract the second number in parts. But in the first problem, I'd change 5,198 to 5,200 because it's just easy."

A student explains how he changed the numbers in a subtraction problem and how he has to compensate to get the final result.

Ask the class to respond to the ideas offered by their classmates. As time allows, ask students who favor one particular strategy to try a different strategy on one of the problems.

Remind students to think about using different strategies as they continue working in the Math Workshop.

ASSESSMENT ACTIVITY

2 Subtraction Problems

15 MIN INDIVIDUALS

At some point during the second half of today's Math Workshop, call students together and tell them to complete the assessment individually. ❶ Students solve two subtraction problems, 793 − 325 and 12,100 − 510, on Assessment: Subtraction Problems (M15). They are expected to use an efficient strategy to solve each problem accurately, and to use clear and concise notation. This assessment focuses on Benchmark 2. As students finish, they can return to Math Workshop activities.

Professional Development

❶ **Teacher Note:** Assessment: Subtraction Problems, p. 132

Name _____ Date _____
Thousands of Miles, Thousands of Seats

Assessment: Subtraction Problems

Solve these two problems. Record your solutions clearly and concisely.

1. 793 − 325 =

2. 12,100
   − 510

Session 2.5 — Unit 3 **M15**

▲ **Resource Masters, M15**

Name _____ Date _____
Thousands of Miles, Thousands of Seats — Homework

Distance Problems (page 1 of 2)

The Pascal Moving Company moves people from Chicago, Illinois, to other parts of the United States. Use the mileage chart below to answer the following questions. The map of the United States on page 25 is a useful tool. Show all your work. Remember that all trips begin in Chicago.

NOTE Students solve subtraction problems involving distances between cities.

City	Distance (in miles) from Chicago IL	City	Distance (in miles) from Chicago IL
Miami, FL	1,377	Seattle, WA	2,072
Phoenix, AZ	1,800	San Francisco, CA	2,148

1. Tyler is driving to Miami. He has driven 888 miles. How far is he from Miami?

Session 2.5 — Unit 3 **45**

▲ **Student Activity Book, p. 45**

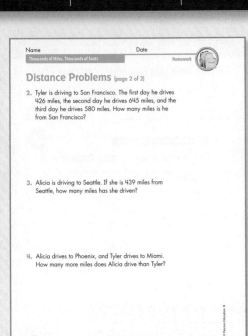

▲ Student Activity Book, p. 46

MATH WORKSHOP
③ Using Subtraction Strategies

30 MIN

Students continue solving subtraction problems. Students should spend most of their time on starter problems (Activity 3B) and distance problems (Activity 3C). This workshop provides you with time to work with individuals or small groups of students, helping them solidify strategies. As students work on the distance and starter problems, continue emphasizing clear and concise notation.

3A The U.S. Algorithm
INDIVIDUALS

For a full description of this activity, see Session 2.4, pages 76–78.

3B More Starter Problems
INDIVIDUALS

For a full description of this activity, see Session 2.3, pages 70–71.

3C More Distance Problems
INDIVIDUALS

For a full description of this activity, see Session 2.2, pages 66–68 and Session 2.4, page 80.

SESSION FOLLOW-UP
④ Daily Practice and Homework

 Daily Practice: For ongoing review, have students complete *Student Activity Book* page 43.

 Homework: Students work on more subtraction problems involving distances on *Student Activity Book* pages 45–46.

 **Student Math Handbook:** Students and families may use *Student Math Handbook* pages 10–13 for reference and review. See pages 149–151 in the back of this unit.

Mathematical Emphases

The Base-Ten Number System Extending knowledge of the number system to 100,000 and beyond

Math Focus Points

◆ Reading, writing, and sequencing numbers to 10,000 and 100,000

Computational Fluency Adding and subtracting accurately and efficiently

Math Focus Points

◆ Adding and subtracting multiples of 100 and 1,000

◆ Solving addition and subtraction problems with large numbers by focusing on the place value of the digits

◆ Solving whole-number addition and subtraction problems efficiently

◆ Using clear and concise notation for recording addition and subtraction strategies

◆ Interpreting and solving multistep problems

Adding and Subtracting Large Numbers

	Student Activity Book	Student Math Handbook	Professional Development: Read Ahead of Time	
SESSION 3.1 p. 88				
Assessment: Division Facts and Close to 7,500 In a variation of *Close to 1,000,* students add 3-digit or 4-digit numbers to get a sum as close to 7,500 as possible.	47–49	8–9; G3	• **Teacher Note:** Learning and Assessing Division Facts Related to Multiplication Combinations to 12 × 12, p. 131	
SESSION 3.2 p. 93				
Stadium Data Students add multiples of 100 and 1,000 to and subtract them from 5-digit numbers. They continue thinking about place value as they solve problems with large numbers.	51–57	8–9, 10–13		
SESSION 3.3 p. 97				
Assessment: Numbers to 100,000 and Rock On! Students focus on what they know about place value and the operations of addition and subtraction to help them solve problems with large numbers. Students are assessed on their ability to read, write, and sequence numbers to 100,000.	51, 59–65	7, 8–9, 10–13; G3		
SESSION 3.4 p. 105				
Rock On!, *continued* Students continue to solve problems with large numbers. The assessment on numbers to 100,000 is completed. During discussion, students share strategies for solving addition and subtraction problems with large numbers.	51, 59–63, 67–68	7, 8–9, 10–13; G3		
SESSION 3.5 p. 110				
End-of-Unit Assessment Students are assessed on the work they have done in this unit on subtracting large numbers.	69	8–9, 10–13	• **Assessment in This Unit,** p. 14 • **Teacher Note:** End-of-Unit Assessment, p. 137	

Practicing Place Value
- No materials needed

Estimation and Number Sense: Closest Estimate
- T38, *Closest Estimate* (page 3 of 3) 🖥

Materials to Gather	Materials to Prepare
• **Digit Cards** (1 deck per pair; from Session 1.3) • **T21–T23, Digit Cards** (from Session 1.3) 🖥 • **T40, *Close to 7,500* Recording Sheet** 🖥	• **M16, *Close to 7,500* Recording Sheet** Make copies. (1 per student plus extras for the Math Workshops in this Investigation) • **M17, *Close to 7,500*** Familiarize yourself with the game rules and make copies. (as needed) • **M18, Assessment: Division Facts** Make copies. (1 per student)
• **T41, Stadium and Arena Capacities** 🖥	
• **M3, Assessment Checklist: Numbers to 100,000** (several copies per class; from Session 1.2) ☑ • **Digit Cards** (1 deck per pair; from Session 1.3) • **M16, *Close to 7,500* Recording Sheet** (as needed; from Session 3.1) • **M17, *Close to 7,500*** (as needed; from Session 3.1) • **12˝ x 18˝ piece of construction paper or blank overhead transparencies** (several per class) • **Folder** (1 per class; optional)	
• **M3, Assessment Checklist: Numbers to 100,000** (several copies per class; from Session 1.2) ☑ • **Digit Cards** (1 deck per pair; from Session 1.3) • **M16, *Close to 7,500* Recording Sheet** (as needed; from Session 3.1) • **M17, *Close to 7,500*** (as needed; from Session 3.1) • **Paper charts or transparencies prepared by volunteers** (from Session 3.3) • **Folder** (1 per class; from Session 3.3; optional)	
	• **M20, End-of-Unit Assessment** Make copies. (1 per student)

🖥 Overhead Transparency   ☑ Checklist Available

Assessment: Division Facts and *Close to 7,500*

Math Focus Points

◆ Solving addition and subtraction problems with large numbers by focusing on the place value of the digits

Today's Plan		Materials
① ACTIVITY **Close to 7,500**	🕐 35 MIN 👥 PAIRS	• *Student Activity Book*, p. 47 • Digit Cards (from Session 1.3); M16 (as needed)*; M17 (as needed)*; T21–T23; T40 🖨
② DISCUSSION **Comparing Strategies**	🕐 15 MIN 👥 CLASS	
③ ASSESSMENT ACTIVITY **Division Facts**	✔ 🕐 10 MIN 👤 INDIVIDUALS	• M18
④ SESSION FOLLOW-UP **Daily Practice and Homework**		• *Student Activity Book*, pp. 48–49 • *Student Math Handbook*, pp. 8–9; G3

*See *Materials to Prepare*, p. 87.

Ten-Minute Math

Practicing Place Value Say "eighty-nine thousand, five hundred sixty-three" and have students write the number. Make sure that all students can read, write, and say this number correctly. Ask students to solve these problems mentally, if possible:

- What is 89,563 + 300? 89,563 + 800? 89,563 + 3,000? 89,563 − 10,000? 89,563 − 12,000?

Write each answer on the board. Ask students to compare each sum or difference with 89,563.

- Which places have the same digits? Which do not? Why?

If time remains, pose additional similar problems using these numbers: 91,002 and 78,410.

① ACTIVITY
Close to 7,500

35 MIN   PAIRS

Remind students of the game they played earlier in the unit, *Close to 1,000.* On the board, write the name of the new game, *Close to 7,500.*

In *Close to 7,500,* instead of adding numbers to try to get close to 1,000, you're going to add numbers to try to get close to 7,500. As you play, think about the strategies you're using.

For this variation, students draw ten Digit Cards instead of eight for each round and make either two 4-digit numbers or a 4-digit number and a 3-digit number whose total is as close to 7,500 as possible. Similar to *Close to 1,000,* the score is the difference between the sum and 7,500 and is recorded on *Student Activity Book* page 47. (Use M16 to make extra copies.)

Demonstrate the game by playing a round or two with the whole class, using transparent Digit Cards (T21–T23) and the transparency of the *Close to 7,500* Recording sheet (T40).

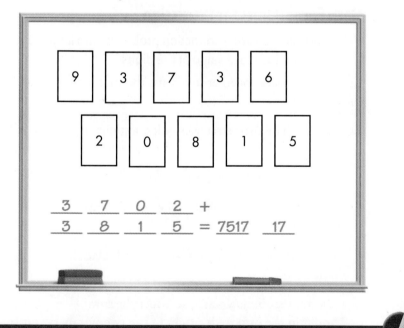

ONGOING ASSESSMENT: Observing Students at Work ✓

Students add two numbers together to get as close to 7,500 as possible.

- **Are students able to use strategies from *Close to 1,000* that also work for *Close to 7,500* (e.g., in *Close to 1,000,* students often look for digits that add up to 10 for the ones place and digits that add up to 9 for tens and hundreds places)?**

▲ **Student Activity Book, p. 47; Resource Masters, M16; T40** 🖶

▲ **Resource Masters, M17**

Teaching Note

❶ **Strategies for *Close to 7,500*** When playing *Close to 1,000*, many students think about the digits in each place separately. In *Close to 7,500*, they need to think more carefully about how the digits they place in the hundreds place affect the number of thousands in the sum. At first, some students may focus on making a sum of 7 with the digits in the 1,000s place and a sum of 5 with the digits in the 100s place. However, using only this strategy limits flexibility and makes it difficult to use larger digits. As you observe students play, help them consider what happens if, for example, they use 9 and 5 in the 100s place. What effect will this have on the 100s place and on the 1,000s place in the sum? What other digits would they look for to put in the 1,000s place of the two addends? If, after a few rounds, students are always trying to make sums of 7 in the 1,000s place and 5 in the 100s place, choose some digit cards for them, such as the following, and ask them what digit they would want for each 1,000s place:

_____ 9 7 0 + _____ 5 3 0

- **Do students use some new strategies for this game (e.g., thinking of 7,500 as 6,000 + 1,500) when choosing digits for the hundreds place?**

- **Are students able to accurately add numbers in the thousands?** Do they break the numbers apart into manageable pieces and recombine them accurately?

DIFFERENTIATION: Supporting the Range of Learners

Intervention Some students will need to continue playing with smaller numbers before they try the game with a larger number. Suggest that these students play a round of *Close to 1,000* and then change the game to a larger number of their choice, such as 1,500 or 2,500.

DISCUSSION

② Comparing Strategies

15 MIN | CLASS

Math Focus Points for Discussion

◆ Solving addition and subtraction problems with large numbers by focusing on the place value of the digits

Call the class back together to discuss the strategies they used to play *Close to 7,500.*

As students share their strategies, ask questions such as the following to help them highlight how they used place value to play the game:

- What strategies did you use?

- How did you use the place value of the digits to help you choose numbers?

- Did you think about each place? Which place did you think about first?

- How did the digits you chose affect the sum? (For example, using 7 and 8 in the hundreds places of the two numbers contributes 1,500 to the sum.)❶

Tell students that they will have a chance to solve problems with larger numbers in the next couple of sessions and that they will come back to this game in a Math Workshop later in the investigation.

ASSESSMENT ACTIVITY
③ Division Facts

10 MIN INDIVIDUALS

Students have been practicing division problems related to the multiplication combinations to 12 × 12, the division facts, throughout this unit. This is the final assessment on these division problems for the year. However, depending on the results of this assessment, you may find that some students may still need to practice a few or perhaps many problems as the school year continues. These students may retake this assessment at a later date, after they have had time for more practice. All students will have opportunities to continue to practice, review, and, most importantly, use these division facts as they solve more division problems throughout the year.❷

This assessment addresses Benchmark 3 of this unit: Demonstrate fluency with division problems related to the multiplication combinations to 12 × 12 (division facts).

In order to meet the benchmark, students should be able to solve 30 division problems (representative of the set of division facts to 144 ÷ 12) accurately in about two minutes. Students who take longer than this but solve all but one or two problems accurately partially meet the benchmark. Students who need a great deal of time to work the problems out in some way, or who give wrong answers for many problems, do not meet the benchmark.

Tell students to solve the problems on Assessment: Division Facts (M18) as quickly as they can, and let them know that you are trying to help them identify which problems they know easily and which they might still have to work on, if any. You can structure this assessment so that you and the students get as much information as possible and so that students do not get frustrated by not being allowed to finish. One method teachers have used is to have students complete as many problems as they can in two minutes by answering the ones they "just know" first. At the end of two minutes, they stop and circle the problems they have not yet solved. Then they continue and solve these problems. This way, you have a record of which problems they needed more time to complete.

Timing can make some students anxious, so talk with students directly about why you want them to solve as many as they can in two minutes and about how that will help you know which problems they still need to work on. If needed, take some time to debrief students about how they felt while they were doing the assessment and what helps them figure out which problems they can tackle if they start to feel anxious.

Professional Development

❷ **Teacher Note:** Learning and Assessing Division Facts Related to Multiplication Combinations to 12 × 12, p. 131

Name		Date
Thousands of Miles, Thousands of Seats		✔

Assessment: Division Facts

21 ÷ 3 =	24 ÷ 4 =	36 ÷ 6 =
48 ÷ 8 =	70 ÷ 10 =	36 ÷ 9 =
42 ÷ 7 =	54 ÷ 9 =	96 ÷ 12 =
35 ÷ 7 =	18 ÷ 6 =	45 ÷ 9 =
77 ÷ 11 =	81 ÷ 9 =	49 ÷ 7 =
64 ÷ 8 =	110 ÷ 11 =	144 ÷ 12 =
54 ÷ 6 =	42 ÷ 6 =	36 ÷ 4 =
48 ÷ 6 =	84 ÷ 7 =	72 ÷ 8 =
11)121	9)27	7)63
8)56	7)28	4)32

M18 Unit 3   Session 3.1

▲ **Resource Masters, M18** PORTFOLIO

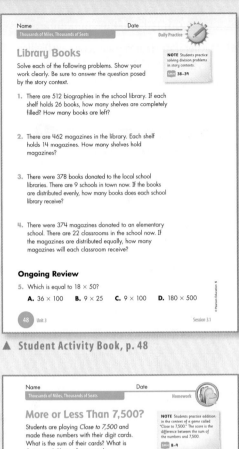

▲ Student Activity Book, p. 48

ONGOING ASSESSMENT: Observing Students at Work

Students demonstrate fluency with multiplication combinations.

- **Are students able to accurately solve division facts problems that are presented in a random order?**

- **Are there particular categories of problems with which students need more practice (e.g., the square number problems or the ÷8 or ÷9 problems)?**

DIFFERENTIATION: Supporting the Range of Learners

Intervention The assessment sheet may be cut apart so that students solve fewer problems at one time. Many students will know the majority of these problems at this point, but some students may need an opportunity to either take this assessment more than once or to continue practicing a few facts that can be assessed individually later on.

SESSION FOLLOW-UP

4 Daily Practice and Homework

 Daily Practice: For ongoing review, have students complete *Student Activity Book* page 48.

Homework: Students practice addition by solving given rounds of *Close to 7,500* on *Student Activity Book* page 49.

Student Math Handbook: Students and families may use *Student Math Handbook* pages 8–9 and G3 for reference and review. See pages 149–151 in the back of this unit.

▲ Student Activity Book, p. 49

Stadium Data

Math Focus Points

◆ Adding and subtracting multiples of 100 and 1,000

◆ Solving addition and subtraction problems with large numbers by focusing on the place value of the digits

◆ Interpreting and solving multistep problems

Today's Plan		Materials
① ACTIVITY **Using Stadium Data**	45 MIN CLASS INDIVIDUALS	• *Student Activity Book*, pp. 51–55 • T41
② DISCUSSION **Strategies with Larger Numbers**	15 MIN PAIRS CLASS	• *Student Activity Book*, p. 52
③ SESSION FOLLOW-UP **Daily Practice and Homework**		• *Student Activity Book*, pp. 56–57 • *Student Math Handbook*, pp. 8–9, 10–13

Ten-Minute Math

Practicing Place Value Write on the board 32, 943 = 32 thousands + 9 hundreds + 4 tens + 3 ones. Ask students to fill in the blanks in the following sums for 32,943 and explain how they figured it out: 30 thousands + _____ hundreds + 43; 28 thousands + _____ hundreds + 43; 49 hundreds + _____ thousands + 43. Write on the board 78,005 = 78 thousands + 5 ones. Ask students to write 5 different combinations of place values that equal 78,005. (For example, 74 thousands, 40 hundreds, 5 ones; 72 thousands, 60 hundreds, 5 ones)

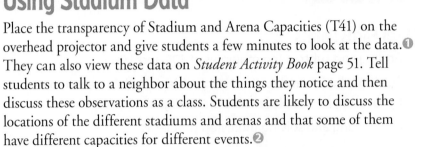

Teaching Note

❶ **Stadium Data** The stadiums used in this investigation are fictional—both the names and the capacities. If there is a stadium in your area with which students are familiar, you may want to refer to it and use it as a visual reference point for size and capacity.

Differentiation

❷ **English Language Learners** While English Language Learners may have attended sporting events, concerts, or other activities in *stadiums* or *arenas,* these words may be unfamiliar to them in English. To prepare English Language Learners to participate fully in the introductory discussion, you can meet in a small group to talk about stadiums and arenas prior to the activity. Bring in some pictures of stadiums and arenas and ask students if they have ever been to one, what kind of events take place there, how many people they think attended, and so on. Make a list of any vocabulary that might be helpful as students explain the data on the *Stadium and Arena Capacities* charts and develop story contexts later in the activity.

Name   Date
Thousands of Miles, Thousands of Seats

Stadium and Arena Capacities

The following tables show the seating capacities of a number of fictitious stadiums and arenas. You will need these data to complete pages 52–55 and pages 59–62.

Football and Baseball Stadiums		
Grand Canyon Stadium	Tempe, AZ	73,521
Garden State Stadium	East Rutherford, NJ	78,741
Gopherdome	Minneapolis, MN	64,035 (football) 55,883 (baseball) 40,000 (basketball, concerts)
Empire Stadium	New York, NY	57,545
Sunshine Stadium	Los Angeles, CA	56,000
Cajundome	New Orleans, LA	69,703 (football) 20,000 (concerts) 55,675 (basketball) 63,525 (baseball)
Patriot Park	Boston, MA	33,993

Arenas		
Copper State Arena	Phoenix, AZ	19,023
Jersey Arena	East Rutherford, NJ	20,049
Big Apple Arena	New York, NY	19,763
Minutemen Center	Boston, MA	18,624 (basketball) 19,600 (concerts)
Badger Arena	Milwaukee, WI	18,600 (basketball) 20,000 (concerts)
Golden State Arena	Los Angeles, CA	20,000

Sessions 3.2, 3.3, 3.4   Unit 3 **51**

▲ **Student Activity Book, p. 51; Transparencies, T41**

ACTIVITY

1 Using Stadium Data

45 MIN   CLASS   INDIVIDUALS

Place the transparency of Stadium and Arena Capacities (T41) on the overhead projector and give students a few minutes to look at the data.❶ They can also view these data on *Student Activity Book* page 51. Tell students to talk to a neighbor about the things they notice and then discuss these observations as a class. Students are likely to discuss the locations of the different stadiums and arenas and that some of them have different capacities for different events.❷

Students discuss data about stadium capacities, a context for solving addition and subtraction problems with larger numbers.

For the next few days, we're going to be working with these data. These numbers are larger than numbers we've been adding and subtracting in this unit so far, and we're going to decide how working with larger numbers is the same as, and different from, working with smaller numbers.

Ask students about their experiences at these kinds of venues.

Who has been to an event in a large space? What kind of event? When people go to these events, when do they show up? All at the same time? Early? Right on time? Late? Do people ever leave early? Why?

Students use the stadium data to solve problems individually on *Student Activity Book* pages 52–55.❸ Tell students that as they complete the pages, they should think about how the work they have done so far (with the 10,000 charts, subtraction strategies and related problems, and *Close to 7,500*) helps them think about computing larger numbers. Also tell them that the problems on page 52 will be discussed after most students have finished them.

ONGOING ASSESSMENT: Observing Students at Work

Students add multiples of 100 and 1,000 to and subtract them from 5-digit numbers.

- **How are students solving the problems?** Are they using place value to help them find each answer? If they have to add 1,000 to 57,545, do they know that all the digits in the sum except the digit in the thousands place will be the same as the digits in 57,545? Do they know that the digit in the thousands place in the sum will be one more than the 7 in 57,545?

- **Are students able to recognize which problems are addition situations and which are subtraction?** Do they accurately write equations for these problems?

- **Can students keep track of each part of these multistep problems, and can they use the result of one part in the next part?**

DIFFERENTIATION: Supporting the Range of Learners

Intervention Some students will find it difficult to read the charts on *Student Activity Book* page 51. Help them, or have another student help them, find the numbers they need to solve the problems on pages 52–55. Although the size of the number might make a difference, so might the "friendliness" of the number. Some students might benefit from working with numbers such as 20,000 and adding or subtracting only multiples of 1,000. The number line is also a useful representation for students to see how the numbers change as they add and subtract multiples of 100 and 1,000.

Extension You may want to ask some students to research the real capacities of known stadiums. Have them hold onto this data, because they may want to use it in Sessions 3.3 and 3.4 when students make up their own stadium problems.

DISCUSSION
2 Strategies with Larger Numbers

15 MIN   PAIRS   CLASS

Math Focus Points for Discussion

- Adding and subtracting multiples of 100 and 1,000
- Solving addition and subtraction problems with large numbers by focusing on the place value of the digits

Teaching Note

❸ Reading and Interpreting Multistep Problems
Part of solving problems that are presented in a story context is understanding the problem situation—what the actions of the story are, what information is provided, and what students are being asked to figure out. Give attention to helping students interpret the language of the problems. For example, phrases such as "all but 1,500 people" or "not there yet" might be unfamiliar to some students. Encourage students to work with one another to carefully interpret the problem before rushing to do something with the numbers. Spend time with individuals or small groups and ask them to tell you what is going on in the story and what they are trying to find out. Simple sketches can also be useful. For example, here is a possible sketch for Problem 3:

▲ Student Activity Book, pp. 52–55

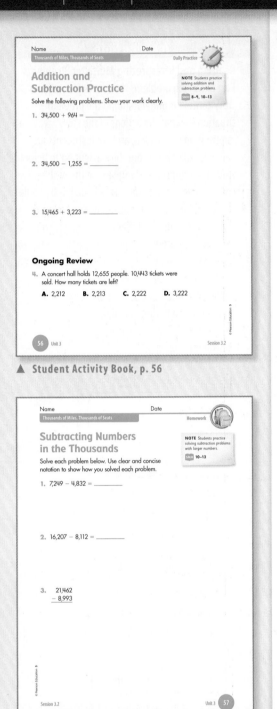

▲ Student Activity Book, p. 56

▲ Student Activity Book, p. 57

This discussion should take place after most students have completed *Student Activity Book* page 52. If many students are having difficulty, have the discussion sooner. If they seem to be doing fine, have the discussion at the end of the session.

Have students share with a partner how they solved Problems 1–3 on page 52. Tell them to focus on how their understanding of the value of the digits in each place helped them solve the problem. Give students 5 minutes or so to discuss this, and then call the class back together.

The computation in these problems is fairly straightforward, as students add or subtract multiples of 1,000. The difficult part of solving Problem 1 (20,000 − 9,000), Problem 2a (9,000 + 5,000), and Problem 2b (20,000 − 14,000) may be keeping track of the parts of the problem and how they build on one another. Note that the answers to these problems are not needed to solve Problem 3.

Ask students to explain their solutions to Problems 1–3. Focus on how they knew what problem they needed to solve and also on how they used place value to solve the problem. Ask questions such as the following:

• How many people are going to the event?

• What information do you already have?

• What information do you still need?

• How does using place value help you solve the problem?

• [Hana] thinks that when you solve Problem 2b (20,000 − 14,000), you can just think 20 − 14 and then remember that it's 6 thousands. Is that true?

If you did not have this discussion at the end of the class, tell students that they have the remainder of the session to complete the other problems.

SESSION FOLLOW-UP

Daily Practice and Homework

 Daily Practice: For reinforcement of this unit's content, have students complete *Student Activity Book* page 56.

 Homework: Students solve subtraction problems on *Student Activity Book* page 57.

Student Math Handbook: Students and families may use *Student Math Handbook* pages 8–9, 10–13 for reference and review. See pages 149–151 in the back of this unit.

Assessment: Numbers to 100,000 and Rock On!

Math Focus Points

◆ Solving whole-number addition and subtraction problems efficiently

◆ Using clear and concise notation for recording addition and subtraction strategies

◆ Interpreting and solving multistep problems

◆ Reading, writing, and sequencing numbers to 10,000 and 100,000

Today's Plan		Materials
① DISCUSSION **Solving Problems with Large Numbers**	15 MIN CLASS PAIRS	• *Student Activity Book*, p. 51 (from Session 3.2)
② MATH WORKSHOP **Adding and Subtracting Large Numbers** **②A** *Rock On!* **②B** *Close to 7,500* **②C** *Make Your Own Story* **②D** Assessment: Numbers to 100,000	45 MIN	**②A** • *Student Activity Book*, p. 51 (from Session 3.2); pp. 59–62 • 12″ x 18″ piece of construction paper or blank overhead transparencies (several per class) **②B** • Materials from Session 3.1, p. 88 **②C** • *Student Activity Book*, p. 63 • Folder (optional) **②D** • M3 (from Session 1.2) ☑
③ SESSION FOLLOW-UP **Daily Practice and Homework**		• *Student Activity Book*, pp. 64–65 • *Student Math Handbook*, pp. 7, 8–9, 10–13; G3

Ten-Minute Math

Estimation and Number Sense: Closest Estimate Show Problems 13–15 on *Closest Estimate* (T38) one at a time. Give students 30 seconds to look at the possible estimates and determine which is the closest to the actual answer. How did you break the numbers apart? How did you determine the magnitude of your answer? If you changed the numbers in the problem, how did you change them and why? Is the closest estimate greater than or less than the actual answer? How do you know?

Teaching Note

❶ **Combining Mental Arithmetic with Recording**
Students have been encouraged to learn to write complete notation clearly so that they can communicate their solutions to you or to peers and so that they do not lose track of their procedures. However, when simply solving a problem for themselves, competent users of arithmetic often combine mental arithmetic with the jotting down of intermediate steps. For example, for the problem 69,703 — 55,675, you might subtract 55,000 from 69,000 mentally and jot down 14,000 (so that you do not have to hold it in your head as you do other parts of the problem), then subtract 675 from 703 mentally (using adding up or another method), and then mentally add 28 to the 14,000 that is jotted down to get 14,028. This problem provides an opportunity to show an example of such recording supporting a mental process. It is important for students to learn that a combination of mental and written steps is useful in practice and that they need to make informed decisions about when they should use complete notation for either their own or others' clarity.

Thousands of Miles, Thousands of Seats

**Estimation and Number Sense:
Closest Estimate** (page 3 of 3)

13. $393 \times 5 \approx$	2,000	2,500	3,000
14. $449 \times 7 \approx$	1,500	3,000	4,500
15. $802 \div 5 \approx$	50	100	150
16. $475 \div 6 \approx$	60	70	80
17. $2,562 \div 5 \approx$	50	500	1,000
18. $835 \times 6 \approx$	4,800	5,400	6,000

T38

▲ Transparencies, T38

DISCUSSION

❶ Solving Problems with Large Numbers

15 MIN CLASS PAIRS

Math Focus Points for Discussion

◆ Solving whole-number addition and subtraction problems efficiently

◆ Using clear and concise notation for recording addition and subtraction strategies

Have students look at *Student Activity Book* page 51 to find the capacity of the Cajundome for football games and for basketball games. Ask a student to read the numbers to the class. (69,703 and 55,675)

How many more tickets can be sold for a football game than for a basketball game? If you want, you may work with a partner to figure this out.

Give students several minutes to solve this problem, and then ask volunteers to explain their thinking. As students are explaining, ask questions such as the following:

• How did you decide how to start?

• Did you use landmark numbers to make the problem easier?

• How did you keep track of your work?❶

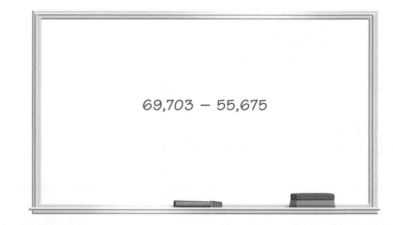

$$69,703 - 55,675$$

Students might say:

"First I ignored the 703 and 675 and figured out that 69,000 — 55,000 is 14,000. Then I had to do 703 — 675. I know that it's 25 from 675 to 700 and then 3 more to 703, so it's 28. So the answer is 14,028."

$$69,000 - 55,000 = 14,000$$
$$14,000 + 28 = 14,028$$

Sample Student Work

Teaching Note

❷ **Combining Strategies** As students solve addition and subtraction problems with large numbers, they are likely to combine strategies. For example, the first student in the Discussion combined subtracting in parts and adding up. At this point in students' work on subtraction, the focus should be on keeping track of what part of the problem they have solved and what remains to be solved.

"I used a number line and added up. I went from 55,675 to 55,700—that's 25. I started to go to 56,000, but then I realized that I could just add 14,000 and be at 69,700, and then I only had to go 3 more."❷

Sample Student Work

"I subtracted in parts by place, so it looked like this."

```
  69,703
 -50,000
 ───────
  19,703
  -5,000
 ───────
  14,703
 -   600
 ───────
  14,103
 -    75
 ───────
  14,028
```

Sample Student Work

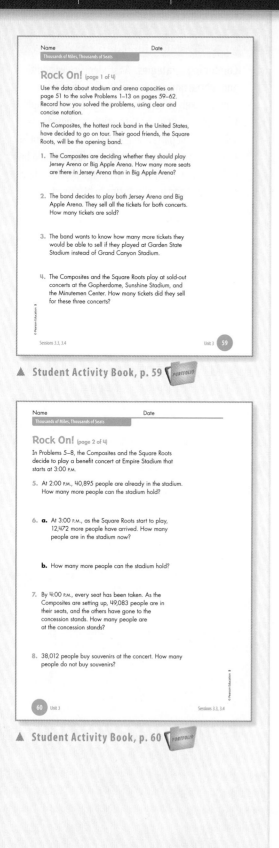

▲ **Student Activity Book, p. 59**

▲ **Student Activity Book, p. 60**

Let students know that for the rest of this session and the next, they are going to solve problems similar to this one in a Math Workshop.

45 MIN

MATH WORKSHOP

② Adding and Subtracting Large Numbers

Students should plan on spending an equal amount of time on each activity. If you think some students would benefit from more work with the 10,000 chart or by solving more *How Many Steps to 10,000?* problems, you may substitute that work for one of these activities. As you work with students, continue reinforcing the idea of clear and concise notation. This Math Workshop continues in the next session.

2A Rock On!

INDIVIDUALS

On *Student Activity Book* pages 59–62, students solve addition and subtraction problems in the context of concerts at different stadiums and arenas.

Like the Filling Up and Emptying problems in yesterday's session, these problems also provide practice solving multistep problems. As students are working, ask them to tell you what is happening in the problem— what they know and what they have to figure out. Encourage students to make quick sketches if that helps them keep track of the steps of the problem. Even a simple sketch such as the following, for Problem 6b, can be useful:

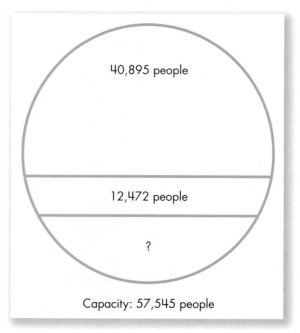

As students are working, find a few students who solve Problem 1 efficiently and with clear notation. Give them either a 12″ x 18″ piece of construction paper or a blank overhead transparency. Ask them to record their work and be prepared to explain it at the beginning of Session 3.4. They might want to practice sharing with another student first. Remind all students to finish the problem by the end of today's session.

ONGOING ASSESSMENT: Observing Students at Work

Students add and subtract large numbers.

- **What strategies are students using to solve these problems?** Do they use knowledge of place value to break numbers apart efficiently?

- **How are students keeping track of their solutions?** How do they know when they are finished? Is their notation clear and concise?

- **Can students interpret what is happening in each step of the problems?** Can they explain what information is given and what they need to figure out?

DIFFERENTIATION: Supporting the Range of Learners

Intervention Interpreting the problems is part of the challenge of solving real-world problems. As needed, work with individuals or small groups of students to talk through and/or sketch what is happening in each part of a problem. Some students will need help keeping track of their work and of the numbers in the problems. To help them record strategies, some students can use the number line as one representation. Some students may need to practice adding or subtracting only multiples of 100 and 1,000. Numbers can be adjusted by using different arenas or by changing the numbers in the problems.

Name _____ Date _____

Thousands of Miles, Thousands of Seats

Rock On! (page 3 of 4)

9. The Composites and Square Roots play at sold-out concerts at Patriot Park and Copper State Arena. How many tickets were sold?

10. The bands sell all but 500 tickets for an 8:00 P.M. concert at Badger Arena. At 7:30 P.M., 18,777 people have arrived. How many people are not at the arena yet?

11. **a.** The bands play at a sold-out concert at Minutemen Center. At 7:00 P.M., 11,456 people are in the arena. At 7:30 P.M., 6,845 more people have arrived. How many people have not shown up?

   b. Everyone has finally arrived at the concert at Minutemen Center. After the Square Roots play, 4,219 people leave their seats to buy refreshments or souvenirs. How many people are still in their seats?

Sessions 3.3, 3.4   Unit 3 61

▲ **Student Activity Book, p. 61** PORTFOLIO

Name _____ Date _____

Thousands of Miles, Thousands of Seats

Rock On! (page 4 of 4)

In Problems 12 and 13, the Composites and the Square Roots play at a sold-out concert at Grand Canyon Stadium that begins at 5:00 P.M.

12. **a.** At 4:00 P.M., 62,106 people are in the stadium. How many more people are expected to show up?

   b. At 4:30 P.M., 10,500 more people have arrived. How many people are at the concert now?

   c. How many people have not yet arrived?

13. As the Composites start to play, everyone has arrived. 64,086 people are in their seats, and the others are at the concession stands. How many people are at the concession stands?

62 Unit 3   Sessions 3.3, 3.4

▲ **Student Activity Book, p. 62** PORTFOLIO

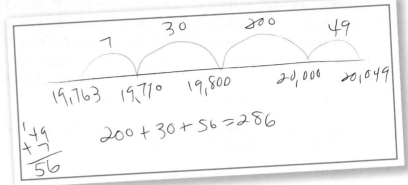

$$200 + 30 + 56 = 286$$

Sample Student Work

$$20,049 - 19,763 = \boxed{286}$$
$$20,000 - 19,000 = 1,000$$
$$1,000 - 763 = 237$$
$$237 + 49 = 286$$

Sample Student Work

$$\begin{array}{r} 33,993 \\ + 19,023 \\ \hline \end{array} \qquad \begin{array}{r} 33,000 \\ + 19,000 \\ \hline 52,000 \end{array} \qquad \begin{array}{r} 993 \\ + 23 \\ \hline 1,016 \end{array}$$

$$52,000 + 1,016 = 53016$$

Sample Student Work

2B Close to 7,500

PAIRS

Students play *Close to 7,500* and think about strategies they can use to help them make sums as close as possible to 7,500. A discussion for this activity is not planned, but you may choose to have a brief whole-/small-group discussion on strategies for winning this game.

For a full description of this activity, see Session 3.1, pages 89–90.

2C Make Your Own Story

INDIVIDUALS

Students use the stadium/arena capacities data to make up their own story of an event and problems that go along with it. They then solve these problems. This work can be compiled into a class book (or put into a folder) for other students to use and solve. Use *Student Activity Book* page 63 to record this story.

DIFFERENTIATION: Supporting the Range of Learners

Extension You may want to ask some students to research the real capacities of known stadiums and use this data to make up their own problems.

2D Assessment: Numbers to 100,000

INDIVIDUALS

Use the Math Workshop today and tomorrow to complete an observed assessment of Benchmark 1: Read, write, and sequence numbers up to 100,000. As students write their own story problems, using numbers up to 100,000, check in with each student for about a minute each. Ask each student to do the following:

- Read two or three numbers up to 100,000

- Write two or three numbers up to 100,000

- Answer two or three questions about sequence, such as "What is the number that is 1 less than the one you just read? What about 1 more? What about 10 less? 100 less?"

Use the second half of Assessment Checklist: Numbers to 100,000 (M3) to record students' responses. (The first half of the checklist was used in Session 1.2.)

Name _____ Date _____

Thousands of Miles, Thousands of Seats

Make Your Own Story

For the past several days, you have been working with the data about stadium and arena capacities on page 51. This is your chance to make up your own story about people coming and going to some sort of event at one of these stadiums or arenas. You should not spend more than 15 minutes writing your story.

1. Decide on an event (concert, game, and so on). _____

2. Decide on a stadium or arena for the event. _____

3. Write 3 to 5 problems about your event.

4. On a separate sheet of paper, solve your own problems.

Sessions 3.3, 3.4   Unit 3   63

▲ Student Activity Book, p. 63

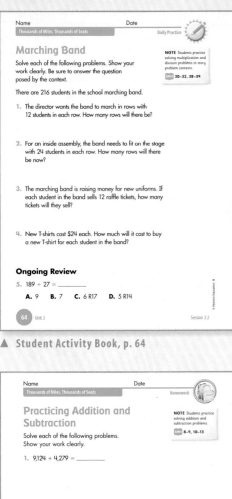

▲ Student Activity Book, p. 64

▲ Student Activity Book, p. 65

SESSION FOLLOW-UP
Daily Practice and Homework

Daily Practice: For ongoing review, have students complete *Student Activity Book* page 64.

Homework: Students solve addition and subtraction problems on *Student Activity Book* page 65.

Student Math Handbook: Students and families may use *Student Math Handbook* pages 7, 8–9, 10–13 and G3 for reference and review. See pages 149–151 in the back of this unit.

Rock On!, *continued*

Math Focus Points

- Solving whole-number addition and subtraction problems efficiently
- Interpreting and solving multistep problems
- Reading, writing, and sequencing numbers to 10,000 and 100,000

Today's Plan		Materials
DISCUSSION ❶ **Strategies for Large Numbers**	🕐 15 MIN 👥 CLASS	• *Student Activity Book,* pp. 59–62 (from Sessions 3.2 and 3.3) • Paper charts or transparencies prepared by volunteers (from Session 3.3)
MATH WORKSHOP ❷ **Adding and Subtracting Large Numbers** **2A** Rock On! **2B** *Close to 7,500* **2C** Make Your Own Story **2D** Assessment: Numbers to 100,000	🕐 45 MIN	**2A** • *Student Activity Book,* pp. 51, 59–62 (from Sessions 3.2 and 3.3) **2B** • Materials from Session 3.1, p. 88 **2C** • *Student Activity Book,* p. 63 (from Session 3.3) • Folder (from Session 3.3; optional) **2D** • M3 (from Session 1.2) ✓
SESSION FOLLOW-UP ❸ **Daily Practice and Homework**		• *Student Activity Book,* pp. 67–68 • *Student Math Handbook,* pp. 7, 8–9, 10–13; G3

Ten-Minute Math

Estimation and Number Sense: Closest Estimate Show Problems 16–18 on *Estimation and Number Sense: Closest Estimate* (T38) one at a time. Give students 30 seconds to look at the possible estimates and determine which is the closest to the actual answer. How did you break the numbers apart? How did you determine the magnitude of your answer? If you changed the numbers in the problem, how did you change them and why? Is the closest estimate greater than or less than the actual answer? How do you know?

DISCUSSION

① Strategies for Large Numbers

Math Focus Points for Discussion

◆ Solving whole-number addition and subtraction problems efficiently

We've been working on adding and subtracting large numbers for a few days now. You were all asked to complete Problem 1 on *Student Activity Book* page 59. Several of your classmates are going to explain their solutions. As they do so, your job is to try to understand what they did and think about how your strategy is the same or different.

Ask the volunteers you identified in Session 3.3 to share the chart or transparency they prepared that shows how they solved Problem 1, 20,049 − 19,763. For each strategy that is explained, ask the student explaining to focus on the following questions:

- How did the numbers in the problem help you choose the strategy you used?

- How did you keep track of the steps in your strategy?

- Did you use just one strategy for this problem, or did you combine strategies?

Students might say:

"I used a number line to add up from 19,763 to 20,049. 19,763 + 37 = 19,800. It's 200 more to 20,000 and then 49 more. Then I added 37 + 200 + 49, and that was 286."

Sample Student Work

"I subtracted back from 20,049 to 19,763. I did 20,049 − 100 = 19,949. Then 19,949 − 100 = 19,849. I couldn't take away another 100, so I did 50; 19,849 − 50 = 19,799. I took away 30 more and then 6 more. Then I added all those numbers up, 100 + 100 + 50 + 36, that was easy. 286!"

$$2\cancel{0}049$$
$$-\quad 100$$
$$\overline{19949}$$
$$-\quad\quad 100$$
$$\overline{19849}$$
$$-\quad\quad 50$$
$$\overline{19799}$$
$$-\quad\quad 30$$
$$\overline{19769}$$
$$-\quad\quad\quad 6$$
$$\overline{19763}$$

Sample Student Work

"The numbers looked close, so I added 300 to 19,763 and got 20,063. That means I added 14 too many, so I had to subtract 14 from 300. That's 286."

$$20049 - 19{,}763$$
$$19{,}763 + 300 = 20{,}063 \quad 63 - 49 = 14$$
$$\text{too much}$$
$$300 - 14 = 286$$

Sample Student Work

At this point, you may choose to have a brief discussion with students about which of the other problems on *Student Activity Book* pages 59–62 look difficult but really are not and which really are difficult. Choose one of each to work through together, as time permits. Also stress that the strategies they have been using all along still work.

Some of you are saying that even though these problems might look difficult because the numbers are large, the same strategies we've been using still work. We can still add up, or subtract one number in parts, or change a number. It also seems that you are finding that adding up or subtracting back to the nearest hundred, thousand, or ten thousand is also very helpful.

MATH WORKSHOP

2 Adding and Subtracting Large Numbers

45 MIN

Students continue the Math Workshop from Session 3.3.

2A Rock On!

INDIVIDUALS

For a full description of this activity, see Session 3.3, pages 100–101.

2B *Close to 7,500*

PAIRS

For a full description of this activity, see Session 3.1, pages 89–90 and Session 3.3, page 103.

2C Make Your Own Story

INDIVIDUALS

For a full description of this activity, see Session 3.3, page 103.

2D Assessment: Numbers to 100,000

INDIVIDUALS

If some students have not yet been assessed, continue with the observed assessment described in Session 3.3 on page 103.

SESSION FOLLOW-UP

3 Daily Practice and Homework

Daily Practice: For ongoing review, have students complete *Student Activity Book* page 67.

Homework: Students solve subtraction problems on *Student Activity Book* page 68.

Student Math Handbook: Students and families may use *Student Math Handbook* pages 7, 8–9, 10–13 and G3 for reference and review. See pages 149–151 in the back of this unit.

Name _____ Date _____

Thousands of Miles, Thousands of Seats

Daily Practice

Mystery Tower

The top part of Felix's multiple tower is shown. Answer these questions about his tower.

NOTE On this page, students practice solving multiplication and division problems.

SMH 20

| 594 |
| 567 |
| 540 |
| 513 |
| 486 |

1. By what number did Felix count? How do you know?

2. How many numbers are in Felix's tower so far? How do you know?

3. Write a multiplication equation that represents how many numbers are in Felix's multiple tower.

   _____ × _____ = _____

4. What is the 10th multiple in Felix's tower? _____

5. Imagine that Felix adds more multiples to his tower.
   a. What would be the 20th multiple in his tower? _____
   How do you know?

   b. What would be the 25th multiple in his tower? _____
   How do you know?

Session 3.4   Unit 3   67

▲ Student Activity Book, p. 67

Name _____ Date _____

Thousands of Miles, Thousands of Seats

Homework

Concert Time

Solve these problems and record your solutions, using clear and concise notation.

NOTE Students practice solving addition and subtraction problems.

SMH 8–9, 10–13

The Composites are playing at a sold-out concert at the Gopherdome, which holds 40,000 people. The concert starts at 8:00 P.M. Answer the questions below and show your work.

1. At 7:00 P.M., 28,175 people are at the concert. How many people have not arrived yet?

2. **a.** By 7:30 P.M., 9,590 more people have arrived. How many people are at the concert now?

   b. How many people have not arrived yet?

3. By 8:00 P.M., all but 1,642 people are at the concert. How many people are at the concert now?

68   Unit 3   Session 3.4

▲ Student Activity Book, p. 68

End-of-Unit Assessment

Math Focus Points

◆ Solving whole-number addition and subtraction problems efficiently

◆ Using clear and concise notation for recording addition and subtraction strategies

Today's Plan		Materials
1 ASSESSMENT ACTIVITY **End-of-Unit Assessment**	✓ 🕐 👤 50 MIN INDIVIDUALS	• M20*
2 DISCUSSION **Solutions to the Assessment Problems**	🕐 👥 10 MIN CLASS	
3 SESSION FOLLOW-UP **Daily Practice**		• *Student Activity Book*, p. 69 • *Student Math Handbook*, pp. 8–9, 10–13

*See *Materials to Prepare*, p. 87.

Ten-Minute Math

Practicing Place Value Write on the board $14,235 = 14,000 + 200 + 30 + 5$. Ask students to fill in the blanks in the following sums for 14,235 and explain how they figured it out: 12 thousands + _____ hundreds + _____ ones; _____ thousands + 52 hundreds + _____ ones.

Write on the board $86,075 = 86,000 + 70$ tens + 5 ones. Ask students to write 5 different combinations of place values that equal 86,075. (For example, 80 thousands, 60 hundreds, and 75 ones.)

ASSESSMENT ACTIVITY

1 End-of-Unit Assessment

50 MIN INDIVIDUALS

This End-of-Unit Assessment (M20) focuses on the second of the unit's benchmarks.❶❷

Benchmark 2: Solve subtraction problems accurately and efficiently, choosing from a variety of strategies.

Problems 1 and 2: Solve two subtraction problems.

At this point in the year, students should have at least one subtraction strategy that they use efficiently, perform accurately, and notate clearly. They should be able to apply these strategies to large numbers. Students should not need the entire 60 minutes to complete this assessment. Consider having some students use this extra time to finish activities from the Math Workshop in this investigation.

ONGOING ASSESSMENT: Observing Students at Work

Students demonstrate their fluency with subtraction as they solve two problems. As students are working, check to make sure that they are communicating their thinking clearly so that you will be able to assess their strategies accurately when you look at their work later.

DIFFERENTIATION: Supporting the Range of Learners

Intervention Ask any students whose work is not clear to explain their thinking to you, and help them notate their strategies. Keep a record of any support you provided and any oral explanations students gave you.

Professional Development

❶ **Assessment in This Unit**, p. 14

❷ **Teacher Note:** End-of-Unit Assessment, p. 137

Name _____ Date _____
Thousands of Miles, Thousands of Seats

End-of-Unit Assessment

Solve these two problems. Record your solutions clearly and concisely.

1. 1,403 − 877 =

2. The capacity of Empire Stadium is 57,545, and the capacity of Patriot Park is 33,993. How many more seats are there in Empire Stadium than in Patriot Park?

M20 Unit 3   Session 3.5

▲ **Resource Masters, M20** PORTFOLIO

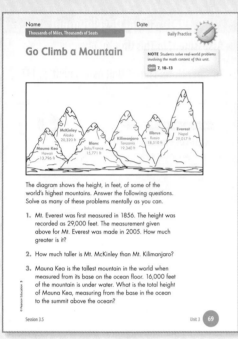

▲ Student Activity Book, p. 69

② Solutions to the Assessment Problems

10 MIN   CLASS

When all students are finished, you may want to have a class discussion about the solutions to the assessment problems.

③ Daily Practice

Daily Practice: For enrichment, have students complete *Student Activity Book* page 69. This page provides real-world problems involving the math content of this unit.

Student Math Handbook: Students and families may use *Student Math Handbook* pages 8–9, 10–13 for reference and review. See pages 148–150 in the back of this unit.

Thousands of Miles, Thousands of Seats

In Part 6 of *Implementing Investigations in Grade 5,* you will find a set of Teacher Notes that addresses topics and issues applicable to the curriculum as a whole rather than to specific curriculum units. They include the following:

Computational Fluency and Place Value

Computational Algorithms and Methods

Representations and Contexts for Mathematical Work

Foundations of Algebra in the Elementary Grades

Discussing Mathematical Ideas

Racial and Linguistic Diversity in the Classroom:
   What Does Equity Mean in Today's Math Classroom?

Place Value

The base-ten number system is a place-value system; that is, any numeral, such as 2, can represent different values, depending on where it appears in a written number: it can represent 2 ones, 2 tens, 2 hundreds, 2 thousands, and so on. Understanding our place-value system requires coordinating the way we write the numerals that represent a particular number (e.g., 5,217) and the way we name numbers in words (e.g., five thousand, two hundred seventeen) with how those numerals represent quantities. (See **Place Value** in *Implementing Investigations in Grade 5.*) In Grade 4, students learned to use and understand numbers in the thousands. In this unit, students revisit their work on numbers up to 10,000 and expand their work to even larger numbers.

The Base-Ten Number System

The heart of the work on place value in Grade 5 is relating the written numerals to the quantity and to how the numerals are composed. Being able to do this is not simply a matter of saying that 5,217 "has 5 thousands, 2 hundreds, 1 ten, and 7 ones," which we know students can easily learn to do without attaching meaning to the quantity these numerals represent. Students must learn to visualize how 5,217 is built up from thousands, hundreds, tens, and ones in a way that helps them relate its value to other quantities. Understanding the place value of a number such as 5,217 entails knowing that 5,217 is closer to 5,000 than to 6,000; that it is 1,000 more than 4,217, 100 more than 5,117, 17 more than 5,200, and 3 less than 5,220; and that it can be decomposed in a number of ways, such as 52 hundreds, 1 ten, and 7 ones.

In this unit, students use 10,000 charts to visualize numbers in the thousands and their relationships. From their work in Grades 3 and 4, students should have a solid understanding of how 1,000 is composed of ten 100s and how each 100 is composed of ten 10s. In Grade 4, students worked with a class 10,000 chart composed of one hundred 100 charts. By building up to 1,000 and then 10,000 from the 100 charts, with which they were very familiar, they learned how these larger numbers are composed. However, because the chart was built from individual 100 charts, the numbering system of each 100 was contained within an individual chart.

In Grade 5, we introduce a different kind of 10,000 chart, in which the dimensions and the numbering system provide a visual image of 10,000 in various ways. The 100 rows with 100 squares in each row provide an image of how 10,000 is composed of one hundred 100s. Each row of the chart contains 100 squares and the rows are numbered 1–100, 101–200, 201–300, and so on. Each group of 10 rows is outlined as a rectangle. Each rectangle contains 10×100, or 1,000, squares. The 10 rectangles provide an image of the composition of 10,000 as 10 groups of 1,000.

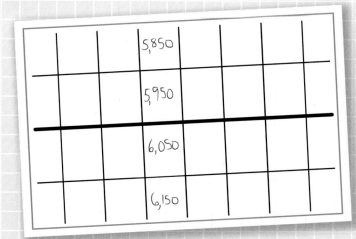

Sample Student Work

Some place-value models, such as base-ten blocks, use three dimensions to help students visualize thousands. We have chosen to continue building on the flat model that students have been using throughout the grades, starting with the 100 chart, which they can now visualize well. In Grade 5, they use new units—rows of 100 and rectangles of 10 hundreds—as the building blocks for composing 10,000.

By using this flat model composed of 100 hundreds, students see all 10,000 squares arranged in a way that helps them visualize the structure of the base-ten system. Through placing numbers on the chart, they consider relationships between numbers. For example, about where would the number 7,927 be? To place this number, students bring into play their knowledge of the relationship of this number to 10,000, to 8,000, to 7,900, and to 7,930. In this process, they are associating the written number with its meaning: the number is in the eighth rectangle, the one that contains the squares numbered 7,001 to 8,000. Because the number is 900 more than 7,000, it is found in the last row of that rectangle, the row that starts with 7,901 and ends with 8,000. It is about a quarter of the way along that row—the 27th square.

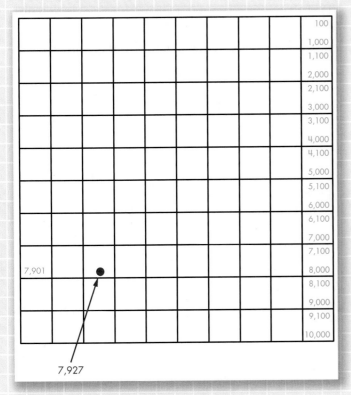

Place Value and Computational Fluency

Students' work on addition and subtraction relates directly to their work on the place-value system. Understanding the place value of each digit in a number leads to an understanding of the magnitude of the number and allows students to estimate what a reasonable answer should be before they carry out any computation. Developing the habits of estimating before computing and of comparing the solution with the estimate is important for all students.

Efficient strategies for solving addition and subtraction problems depend on knowing the addition combinations and their subtraction counterparts and understanding how to add or subtract multiples of 10, 100, 1,000, and so on. Developing fluency with addition and subtraction requires understanding the quantity that digits in any place represent. For example, many students subtract in parts for a problem such as 8,569 − 2,895.

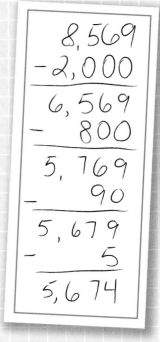

Sample Student Work

In order to carry out this computation, students draw on an understanding of the meaning of each digit. For example, the 2 represents 2,000. Further, they use knowledge about the equivalencies of 1,000 and ten 100s, one 100 and ten 10s, and so on. For example, in the second step of the problem, this student thinks of the first two digits of 6,569 as representing 65 hundreds rather than as 6 thousands and 5 hundreds, allowing the student to subtract 8 hundreds.

Students are also using their knowledge of place value and the basic subtraction "facts" to easily subtract large numbers: $13 - 7 = 6$ (6 ones), $130 - 70 = 60$ (6 tens), $1,300 - 700 = 600$ (6 hundreds). Subtracting 7 from 13 in any place is the same, except that the units that are subtracted are ten times larger in each successive place to the left. In Grade 5, students should be adding or subtracting the largest possible chunks of numbers, rather than counting by 100 or 1,000. Similarly, students are applying other computations they can carry out mentally with numbers below 100 to problems with larger numbers. In the problem above, being able to mentally compute $65 - 8 = 57$ (by subtracting 5 and then 3, for example, or just knowing that $15 - 8 = 7$, so $65 - 8 = 57$) is applied to subtracting 8 hundreds from 65 hundreds.

The strategies for addition used by many students—adding by place or adding on one number in parts—depend on an understanding of how to decompose numbers. (See **Teacher Note:** Addition Strategies on page 116.) The common subtraction strategies of subtracting in parts, adding up, or subtracting back also depend on an understanding of how to decompose numbers. (See **Teacher Note:** Subtraction Strategies on page 119.) The U.S. algorithm for subtraction, which students study in Investigation 2, also depends on a firm grasp of place value.

Addition Strategies

Students' strategies for addition fall into two basic categories, as follows:

1. Breaking the numbers apart, then adding these parts
2. Changing the numbers to numbers that are easier to add

In order to use the strategies described in this **Teacher Note,** students must understand the meaning of addition and have a good mental model of what is happening in the problem. They must be able to look at the problem as a whole, think about the relationships of the numbers in the problem, and choose an approach that they can carry out easily and accurately.

Grade 5 students should be familiar with strategies in each category. They should feel comfortable and confident with more than one strategy and should be able to use each one efficiently; for example, by adding the largest or most reasonable parts of the number and using the fewest number of steps.

Here are examples of students' strategies, using the following problem as an example:

$$8,349 + 4,175 =$$

The steps for each strategy are all written out in this **Teacher Note,** but in practice, students at this grade should be able to carry out many of these steps mentally, jotting down what they need to keep track of partial sums.

Breaking the Numbers Apart

In strategies that involve breaking numbers apart and then adding the parts, students use their understanding of the ways in which numbers can be decomposed to solve the problem.

In Set 1, students break up one of the addends into parts and then add these parts, one at a time, to the other number. Students often call this set of solutions "adding one number in parts."

Set 1: Adding one number in parts

$$8,349 + 4,175 =$$

$8,349 + 4,100 = 12,449$	$8,349 + 4,000 = 12,349$
$12,449 + 70 = 12,519$	$12,349 + 100 = 12,449$
$12,519 + 5 = 12,524$	$12,499 + 50 = 12,499$
	$12,499 + 25 = 12,524$

These two students started with 8,349 but broke 4,175 up in different ways (4,100 + 70 + 5 and 4,000 + 100 + 50 + 25). When students use this strategy, they should be encouraged to add the largest "chunks" of numbers possible while still making sense of the problem and the numbers. For example, the second solution could be carried out more efficiently by adding 150 and then 25. Students often use a number line to represent their thinking when using this strategy.

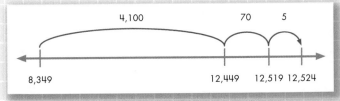

In the solutions in Set 2, students break the numbers apart by place value, add each place, and then find a final total. Students often call these approaches "adding by place."

Set 2: Adding by place

$$8,349 + 4,175 =$$

$$8,000 + 4,000 = 12,000$$
$$300 + 100 = 400$$
$$40 + 70 = 110$$
$$9 + 5 = 14$$

$$\begin{array}{r} \overset{1\,1}{8,349} \\ + 4,175 \\ \hline 12,524 \end{array}$$

$$12,000 + 400 + 110 + 14 = 12,524$$

The first student added by place, starting with the largest place. The second student used the U.S. algorithm (sometimes called "carrying" or regrouping), which is also an example of adding by place. Students studied the U.S. algorithm and compared these two examples in Grade 4 in *Landmarks and Large Numbers*.

Changing the Numbers

In this category of approaches, students change one or both of the numbers to what they often call "landmark" or "friendly" numbers, generally multiples of 10 or 25. In Set 3, students change the numbers to multiples of 10 to create easier addition problems. Students often call this kind of solution "changing to a landmark."

Set 3: Changing the numbers and adjusting the sum

$$8,349 + 4,175 =$$

$$8,350 + 4,175 = 12,525 \qquad 8,349 + 4,200 = 12,549$$
$$12,525 - 1 = 12,524 \qquad 12,549 - 25 = 12,524$$

$$8,350 + 4,200 = 12,550$$
$$12,550 - 25 - 1 = 12,524$$

After students have changed one or both numbers to a landmark and find the sum, they have to decide what to do to the sum to compensate for their initial changes.

The first student added 1 to 8,349 and then had to subtract 1 to get the final answer. The second student used a similar strategy, adding 25 to 4,175 and then subtracting 25 at the end. The third student changed both numbers, added them, and then subtracted both the 25 and the 1 that had been added at the beginning.

Sometimes students change the numbers in an addition problem in such a way that they create an equivalent problem that is easier to solve, as did these two students.

Set 4: Creating an equivalent problem

$$8,349 + 4,175 =$$

$$8,324 + 4,200 = 12,524 \qquad 8,400 + 4,124 = 12,524$$

In these examples, an increase in one addend is matched by an equal decrease in another addend so that no additional adjustment is needed after the total has been found. The first student subtracted 25 from 8,349 and added 25 to 4,175. The second student added and subtracted 51.

Representing Subtraction on the Number Line

When students use a number line to represent the action in a subtraction situation, they may think about it in two different ways. Consider the following problem:

$$1,000 - 485 =$$

Some students look at this problem and think about the question "How far is it from 485 to 1,000?" They may do this if the context of the problem suggests visualizing the problem in this way, or this may simply be their preferred way of thinking about subtraction, regardless of the context. When these students use a number line to represent subtraction problems, they show either adding up in jumps from the smaller number to the larger number or subtracting back in jumps from the larger number to the smaller number.

Finding the Difference by Adding Up

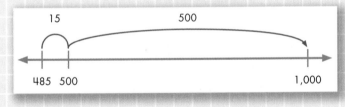

Finding the Difference by Subtracting Back

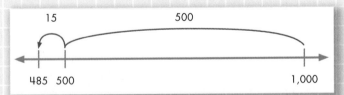

In both of these representations, the jumps represent the distance between the two numbers on the number line: How much more is 1,000 than 485? How much less is 485 than 1,000? Students might notate this conception of the problem as $485 + \_\_\_ = 1,000$ or $1,000 - \_\_\_ = 485$.

Finding the Difference by Taking Away

Other students think of the problem in a different way, and their number line representation is quite different. In this case, students think about the question "If I take away 485 from 1,000, how much is left?" Again, this way of thinking about the problem may be suggested by a particular context, or some students may always solve subtraction problems by thinking about removing one quantity from the other, regardless of context. Their representations on the number line start at the number from which they are going to remove some amount and then show how they "take away" that quantity in parts.

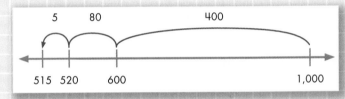

Students might notate this conception of the problem as $1,000 - 485 = \_\_\_$.

The number line representations of both distance and taking away are useful in visualizing subtraction. However, keep in mind that a student thinking about the distance between the two numbers on the number line may not at first understand the representation of the same problem as taking away a quantity, and vice versa.

Make sure that students notice where the solution to the problem is found on each representation. In the first two figures, the difference is seen in the distance (the jumps) between the two numbers on the number line. In the third figure, the difference is the number on the number line on which the student finally lands after making all the jumps. Help students see how each number line representation works and how it connects to a particular way of thinking about subtraction.

Subtraction Strategies

Students' strategies for subtraction fall into 4 basic categories, as follows:

1. Subtracting in parts
2. Adding up or subtracting back from one number to the other
3. Changing the numbers to numbers that are easier to subtract
4. Subtracting by place

In order to use the strategies described in this Teacher Note, students must understand the meaning of subtraction and have a good mental model of what is happening in the problem. They must be able to look at the problem as a whole, think about the relationships of the numbers in the problem, and choose an approach that they can carry out easily and accurately.

At the end of this unit, fifth-grade students should be familiar with strategies in each of these categories. They should feel comfortable and confident with at least one strategy and should be able to use it efficiently, working with the largest or most reasonable parts of the number and using the fewest number of steps.

Here are examples of students' strategies, using the following problem as an example:

$$3,451 - 1,287 =$$

1. Subtracting in Parts

$$3,451 - 1,287 =$$

$3,451 - 1,200 = 2,251$	$3,451 - 1,000 = 2,451$
$2,251 - 80 = 2,171$	$2,451 - 100 = 2,351$
$2,171 - 7 = 2,164$	$2,351 - 100 = 2,251$
	$2,251 - 50 = 2,201$
	$2,201 - 30 = 2,171$
	$2,171 - 7 = 2,164$

$$
\begin{array}{r}
3,451 \\
-\ 1,000 \\
\hline
2,451 \\
-\ 200 \\
\hline
2,251 \\
-\ 80 \\
\hline
2,171 \\
-\ 7 \\
\hline
2,164
\end{array}
$$

These three students subtracted 1,287 in parts. The first student broke up 1,287 by place (1,200 + 80 + 7), while the second student subtracted 1,000 and then broke up the 200 and the 87. The third student subtracted 1,000 first and 200 second and then broke 87 into 80 + 7. As students use this strategy, encourage them to subtract the largest parts they can use while still making sense of the problem and the numbers. Work with students to gradually subtract larger amounts, for example, subtracting 80 rather than subtracting 50, then 30, or 200 instead of 100 + 100. However, keep in mind that fluent students often quickly subtract smaller parts mentally without the need to write down all the steps. Students sometimes call this strategy "subtracting one number in parts."

2. Adding Up or Subtracting Back

In this category of strategies, students visualize how much more or less one number is than the other and either add up or subtract back to find their answer. They often represent the subtraction as the distance between two numbers on a number line. In Set 1, students start at 1,287 and add up until they reach 3,451.

Set 1: Adding up

$$3,451 - 1,287 =$$

$$
\begin{array}{ll}
1,287 + 13 = 1,300 & \qquad 1,287 + 2,000 = 3,287 \\
1,300 + 2,151 = 3,451 & \qquad 3,287 + 100 = 3,387 \\
13 + 2,151 = 2,164 & \qquad 3,387 + 13 = 3,400 \\
 & \qquad 3,400 + 51 = 3,451 \\
 & \qquad 2,000 + 100 + 13 + 51 = 2,164
\end{array}
$$

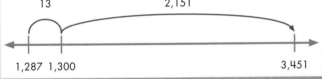

Both students thought of the solution as how much more must be added to 1,287 to get a sum of 3,451. Implicitly, they are using the inverse relationship of addition and subtraction to solve the problem. As shown on the number line, the first student added 13 to 1,287 to get to 1,300 and then added 2,151 to get to 3,451. The second student looked for the largest multiple of 1,000, the largest multiple of 100, and then the largest multiple of 10. Students often call this strategy "adding up."

In Set 2, students started at 3,451, and then subtracted back until they reached 1,287.

Set 2: Subtracting back

$$3,451 - 1,287 =$$

$$
\begin{array}{ll}
3,451 - 51 = 3,400 & \qquad\quad 3,451 \\
3,400 - 2,100 = 1,300 & \qquad\quad \underline{-\ 2,151} \\
1,300 - 13 = 1,287 & \qquad\qquad\ \, 1,300 \\
 & \qquad\qquad \underline{-\quad 13} \\
51 + 2,100 + 13 = 2,164 & \qquad\qquad\ \, 1,287
\end{array}
$$

$$2,151 + 13 = 2,164$$

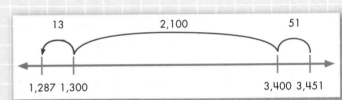

Both students solved the problem by "going back" to 1,300 and then "back 13 more" to 1,287. The first student took three steps; the second student did it in two. As you can see in the number line representation, students are not subtracting 1,287 in parts as in the first category; rather, they start at 3,451, subtract until they reach 1,287, and then determine how much they subtracted. Students often describe this method as figuring out "how far" 1,287 is from 3,451.

3. Changing the Numbers

In this group of strategies, students change one or both of the numbers to what they often call "landmark" or "friendly" numbers. In Set 3, students changed one or both of the numbers, subtracted, and then compensated for the changes they had made.

Set 3: Changing and compensating

$$3,451 - 1,287 =$$

$$3,451 - 1,300 = 2,151 \qquad 3,450 - 1,300 = 2,150$$
$$2,151 + \quad 13 = 2,164 \qquad 2,150 + \quad 14 = 2,164$$

The first student changed 1,287 to 1,300 to create an easier subtraction problem. Because she had subtracted 13 too much, 13 was then added to 2,151 to get the final answer. The second student changed both numbers and had to decide how both those changes affected the result. Because the difference between the two numbers was decreased by 1 (changing 3,451 to 3,450) and by 13 (changing 1,287 to 1,300), 14 is added to 2,150. Visualizing the effect of the changes and, therefore, how to compensate for those changes is critical to this kind of strategy. Number lines are particularly useful tools for visualizing how changing numbers affects the result. The figure in the next column shows the differences between 1,300 and 3,450 and between 1,287 and 3,451 as distances on the number line. In this case, changing 1,287 to 1,300 *and* changing 3,451 to 3,450 make the distance smaller.

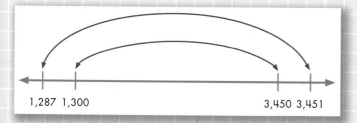

1,287 1,300 .... 3,450 3,451

In general, we do not encourage students to change both numbers in a subtraction problem, as Mitch did in the example on this page. If a student can indeed visualize what these changes mean and how to adjust the result to get the answer to the original problem, then that student can certainly use this method when it makes sense for a particular problem. However, too many students change both numbers to "easy" numbers without a clear idea of how those changes affect the difference.

Classroom experience indicates that thinking through how to adjust the result after changing only one number in a subtraction problem can be challenging for Grade 5 students. Discussions of this idea have been very fruitful in helping students think more deeply about the operation of subtraction and the relationship between the two numbers in a subtraction expression, whether or not students actually use this method to solve problems.

Set 4 is an example of changing both numbers in order to create an equivalent problem that can then be solved without any need to compensate for changes.

Set 4: Making an equivalent problem

$$3,451 - 1,287 =$$

$$1,287 + 13 = 1,300$$
$$3,451 + 13 = 3,464$$

$$3,451 - 1,287 = 3,464 - 1,300 = 2,164$$

This student created an equivalent problem that is easier to solve by adding 13 to both numbers. Adding or subtracting the same quantity to or from both numbers maintains the difference. You might visualize transforming the problem in this way as sliding the difference along a number line:

1,287 1,300 .... 3,451 3,464

Although it is not surprising for students to use this strategy, it is not as common as the others listed here. It is not explicitly mentioned in the text of this investigation, but it may come up in your classroom.

4. Subtracting by Place

Adding by place (adding ones to ones, tens to tens, hundreds to hundreds, and so on) is one of the addition strategies most often used by students. However, subtracting by place is not as straightforward. Consider our sample problem.

$$3,451$$
$$- 1,287$$

It is easy to subtract 200 from 400, but how do you subtract 80 from 50 or 7 from 1? The following two strategies are based on subtracting by place value:

$$3,\overset{\overset{1}{3}\overset{4}{4}1}{451}$$
$$- 1,287$$
$$2,164$$

This student's work is the algorithm which has been commonly taught in the U.S. and is sometimes called "borrowing" or regrouping. This algorithm requires recomposing the number 3,451 to make it possible to subtract in each place. The shorthand notation means that 3,451 (3,000 + 400 + 50 + 1) has been recomposed into 3,000 + 300 + 140 + 11, which then allows easy subtraction by place. (Students study this algorithm in Investigation 2.)

Another student's work is a strategy often developed by students who understand that it is possible to subtract, for example, 80 from 50, resulting in −30. Using this method, subtracting by place results in differences for each place, which can be positive or negative. Combining these differences gives the answer to the problem.

$$3,451$$
$$- 1,287$$
$$2,000$$
$$200$$
$$-30$$
$$-6$$
$$2,164$$

$$2,000 + 200 + (-30) + (-6) = 2,164$$

See **Teacher Note:** Why Study the Conventional Algorithms? on page 128 for more information on why the U.S. subtraction algorithm is studied in this unit and what mathematical understandings students need to examine for this, or any, strategy.

Teacher Note

Describing, Comparing, and Classifying Subtraction Strategies

In Investigation 2, students describe and classify their subtraction strategies. They classified both addition and subtraction strategies in Grade 4 and multiplication strategies this year in Unit 1, *Number Puzzles and Multiple Towers*.

Subtraction strategies are classified by the way students start to solve a problem—their first step. The first step generally indicates how they are thinking about the problem.

$$892 - 567 =$$
$$892 - 500 = 392$$
$$392 - 60 = 332$$
$$332 - 7 = 325$$

Shandra's Work

$$892 - 567 =$$
$$567 + 3 = 570$$
$$570 + 30 = 600$$
$$600 + 200 = 800$$
$$800 + 92 = 892$$

$$3 + 30 + 200 + 92 = 325$$

Joshua's Work

To solve $892 - 567$, Shandra starts by subtracting 500 from 892 whereas Joshua starts by adding 3 to 567. Shandra is breaking up 567 by place and subtracting each part, and Joshua is adding up from 567 to 892.

Strategies are made public so that all students can benefit from seeing the different subtraction methods. Students are encouraged to expand their repertoire of strategies so that they continue to become more flexible and fluent in their computation. Comparing different solutions in the same category also offers the opportunity to discuss how to become more efficient in solving problems by adding or subtracting larger "chunks" of the numbers.

Identifying strategies helps students understand the mathematics of their work. As you listen to students explain their strategies, model language they can use to describe their methods by reflecting back to them what they are doing. For example, you might say, "I see that you are breaking up 567 by place," or "Are you adding up from 567?"

Your language can also help students notice similarities between variations of a method: "Renaldo is also adding up from 567, but he decided to add on 300 first." Ask students to compare their methods to those that have been shared, "Who else broke up 567 into parts, then subtracted each part from 892? . . . Yumiko broke up 567 differently from the way Shandra did; she broke it into $2 + 60 + 500 + 5$ because she noticed that she could subtract 2 from 892 as her first step to get to 890, which was an easy number to work with."

Let students decide as a class which methods should be grouped together on one chart and which are different. This work is about helping students make sense of a variety of solutions; it is not about matching their work to predetermined categories. However, you may have to guide the discussion to keep the number of categories reasonable and useful. Variations of similar methods by different students—such as Shandra's and Yumiko's—can go on the same chart.

Some students combine methods. For example, students might start by changing one of the numbers in the problem, then solve the problem by using another method, and then adjust for the change. For example, Hana solved $892 - 567$ this way:

$$892 - 570 =$$
$$892 - 500 = 392$$
$$392 - 70 = 322$$
$$322 + 3 = 325$$

Hana's Work

Hana started by adding 3 to 567 to make it 570, subtracted 570 in two parts, and then adjusted for her initial change by adding 3.

As you discuss strategies, you may want to ask students who are not combining methods to share their methods first so that some clear categories can be established. Then students can decide how to classify a method like Hana's. They might classify it according to its first step as "changing one number to make it easier and then adjusting at the end;" they might make a new chart of "mixed methods;" or they might want to label the variations on the "changing one number" chart with the ways that each is continued. Students and adults who are fluent with computation often use a mixture of methods in the way that Hana does.

Teacher Note

Reasoning and Proof in Mathematics

As students find strategies to perform calculations, they frequently make claims about numerical relationships. Part of the work of fifth grade involves helping students to strengthen their ability to verbalize those claims and consider such questions as: Does this claim hold for all numbers? How can we know? Finding ways to answer these questions will provide the basis for making sense of formal proof when it is introduced in later years. Consider the following vignette in which students in a fifth grade class are developing methods for solving a subtraction problem.

Georgia: Here is what I tried for 1,232 − 196, I did what I do in addition. I changed the 196 to 200. 200 is easy to work with. 1,232 − 200 is 1,032 but now I am wondering if I should add the 4 and get 1,036 for the answer or subtract it to get 1,028.

Teacher: How would it work if you were adding 1,232 and 196?

Georgia: In addition I know I add 4 to one number and subtract 4 from the other and the answer is the same.

Teacher: Are you saying that if this were 1,232 + 196, you would change it to 1,228 + 200 by adding and subtracting 4 and know the answer would be the same?

Charles: You will get the same answer. If you take some number from one and put it on the other, the answer has to stay the same.

Rachel: I remember we used a story about apples to talk about this. It would be like I have 1,232 apples in one bag and 196 apples in another bag. I can take 4 of the apples out of the first bag and put them in the second bag. That means 1,232 + 196 = 1,228 + 200. You still have the same number of apples.

Teacher: Now Georgia is asking what happens if it isn't about addition. What if it is a subtraction problem? If you try to solve 1,232 − 196 by starting with 1,232 − 200, what do you do with the 4? Do you add it or subtract it to get the correct answer?

Georgia: Now I am thinking I should add the 4 to the 1,232 and make the problem 1,236 − 200. That will be the same as 1,232 − 196. Whatever you add to one you have to add to the other. I see it now. It keeps them the same amount apart.

Rachel: I think that will be true all the time for subtraction—you add the same to both.

Teacher: How could you show whether what Rachel says is always true? Let's first be clear about what Rachel is saying.

The teacher asks Rachel to repeat her assertion and writes Rachel's words on the board:

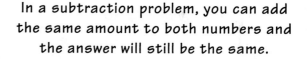

In a subtraction problem, you can add the same amount to both numbers and the answer will still be the same.

Teacher: I'd like you to show whether or not what Rachel is saying is true. You can start by trying some more examples, but then I want you to use a story problem, like Rachel's apple story, or a number line, or some kind of picture to show your thinking. You can use story problems, number lines, or diagrams to show your thinking. Remember, Rachel says this works for all subtraction problems. You have to think about how your explanation works for all numbers.

In this class, Rachel has made an assertion—mathematicians call such an assertion a conjecture—that if you add a certain amount to both numbers in a subtraction problem, the difference remains the same. The teacher has challenged the class to find a way to show that this conjecture is true.

Let us return to the Grade 5 class to see how the students responded to the teacher's challenge to justify their conjecture.

Martin: I made a number line. On the top is 1,232 − 196. The bottom shows 1,236 − 200. You just move the whole thing over 4. It has to be the same.

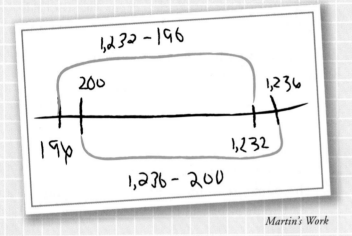

Martin's Work

Kim: I thought of a story. My little sister and I both have penny banks. I have 1,232 pennies and she has 196. To see how many more pennies I have, I'd do 1,232 − 196. But suppose my mom gives us each 4 pennies. Then it would be 1,236 − 200. I still have the same amount more.

Teacher: Kim's story and Martin's number line both show us that 1,232 − 196 = 1,236 − 200. How can we use their work to say this works for all numbers?

Felix: With the number line it doesn't matter what the numbers are at the beginning or the end of the jump. If you move the loop to the right or to the left, the loop stays the same.

Cecelia: It is the same with Kim's story. Whatever is in the penny banks at the beginning, you can add the same number to both of them and the difference would have to be the same.

Kim has used a story context that represents subtraction, in this case a comparison situation, to explain how adding the same amount to both numbers in a subtraction problem will keep the difference the same. Martin has drawn a number line to illustrate the same relationship. Felix then explains how Martin's number line can illustrate any subtraction problem. Similarly Cecelia explains how Kim's story context can apply to all subtraction problems.

Students in Grades K–5 can work productively on developing justifications for mathematical ideas as the students in this class do here. But what is necessary to prove an idea in mathematics? First we'll examine what proving is in the field of mathematics, then we will return to the kind of proving students can do in fifth grade.

What is Proof in Mathematics?

Throughout life, when we make a claim or assertion, we are often required to justify the claim to persuade others that it is valid. A prosecutor who claims that a defendant is guilty of a crime, must make an argument, based on evidence, to convince the jury of this claim. A scientist who asserts that the earth's atmosphere is becoming warmer must marshal evidence, usually in the form of data and accepted theories and models, to justify the claim. Every field, including the law, science, and mathematics, has its own accepted standards and rules for how a claim must be justified in order to persuade others.

In mathematics, a *theorem* must start with a mathematical assertion, which has explicit hypotheses (or "givens") and an explicit conclusion. The proof of the theorem must show how the conclusion follows logically from the hypotheses. A mathematical argument is based on logic and gives a sense of why a proposition is true. For instance, Georgia and Rachel asserted that the difference of two numbers remains the same if you add the same amount to both. In later years, Georgia's statement might be expressed as $(a − b) = (a + n) − (b + n)$. The proof of this claim consists of a series of steps in which one begins with the hypothesis—

a and *b* are numbers—and follows a chain of logical deductions ending with the conclusion—$(a - b) = (a + n) - (b + n)$. Each deduction must be justified by an accepted definition, fact, or principle, such as the commutative and associative laws of addition and the laws describing additive inverses and identities.

The model for such a notion of proof was first established by Euclid, who codified what was known of Ancient Greek geometry in his *Elements,* written about 300 B.C. In his book, Euclid begins with the basic terms of geometry (a point, a line) and their properties (a line is determined by two points) and, through hundreds of propositions and proofs, moves to beautiful and surprising theorems about geometric figures.

What Does Proof Look Like in Fifth Grade?

One does not expect the rigor or sophistication of a formal proof or the use of algebraic symbolism from children in the elementary grades. Even for a mathematician, precise validation is often developed *after* new mathematical ideas have been explored and are more solidly understood. When mathematical ideas are evolving and there is a need to communicate the sense of *why* a claim is true, then informal methods of proving are appropriate. Such methods can include the use of visual displays, concrete materials, or words. The test of effectiveness of such a justification is: Does it rely on logical thinking about the mathematical relationships rather than on the fact that one or a few specific examples work?

An important part of the fifth grader's justification is Felix's statement that it doesn't matter what the numbers are. He understands how Martin's representation of subtraction on the number line could apply to any subtraction situation. In a similar way, Cecelia is able to use the representation of subtraction in Kim's comparison story to reason about other subtraction problems.

Proving, by calling upon a model that represents the operation as these students do, is particularly appropriate in K–5 classrooms where mathematical ideas are generally "under construction," and in which sense-making and diverse modes of reasoning are valued. The fifth graders' argument offers justification for the claim that if you add the same amount to both numbers in a subtraction problem, the difference remains the same. For Kim, the difference is represented by comparing the two amounts in penny banks. Adding the same amount to both banks will not change the difference. Kim's argument not only establishes the validity of the claim for particular numbers, but for any whole numbers, and easily conveys why it is true. Martin's number line diagram offers a visual image for the subtraction situation; the jump represents the difference between any two given numbers.

To support the kind of reasoning illustrated in the vignette, teachers should encourage students to use representations such as cubes, story contexts, or number lines to explain their thinking. The use of representations offers a reference for the student who is explaining his or her reasoning, and it also allows more classmates to follow that reasoning. If it seems that students may be thinking only in terms of specific numbers, teachers might ask,

Will that work for other numbers? How do you know? Will the explanation be the same?

Why Study the U.S. Conventional Algorithms?

In *Investigations*, the algorithms traditionally taught in the United States are studied by students after they have developed their own fluent methods for solving problems with whole numbers in each operation. These include the "carrying" algorithms for addition and multiplication, and the "borrowing" algorithm for subtraction. Historically, these algorithms were developed for doing calculations by hand with a minimum of steps and compact notation. The power of these algorithms for quick calculation lies largely in the fact that they require the user to carry out a series of mostly single-digit calculations. They were designed so that the user could rely on a small set of known number combinations and the repetition of a small sequence of steps to solve any problem. These algorithms, as human inventions, are elegant and efficient.

However, in the elementary grades, when we want students to acquire solid understanding of the base-ten number system and the meaning of arithmetic operations, these algorithms tend to obscure both the place value of digits and the fundamental properties of the operations. Research and practice in the field of mathematics education have shown that there are alternative algorithms and strategies that students develop that help them maintain a focus on understanding place value and the operations.

> "Standard algorithms, in contrast to children's constructed algorithms, are quite far removed from their conceptual underpinnings. They have evolved over centuries for efficiency and compactness. They can be executed quickly, but they can be difficult to learn with understanding." (*Adding It Up*, page 201)

> "Standard multiplication and division algorithms used in the United States are complex procedures in which multiplying alternates with adding or subtracting. . . . In these algorithms the meaning and scaffolding provided by sub-steps have been sacrificed for efficiency. The algorithms use alignment of place value to keep the steps organized without requiring the student to understand what is actually happening with the ones, tens, hundreds, and so on". (*Adding It Up*, page 207)

In this curriculum, students develop strategies that are generalizable and efficient, but that keep the focus on the meaning of the numbers and the operations. Each student may settle on one strategy for each operation that they use most often for routine problems. However, in *Investigations*, students are expected to study more than one algorithm or strategy for each operation. Students study a variety of approaches for the following three reasons:

1. Different algorithms and strategies provide access to analysis of different mathematical relationships.
2. Access to different algorithms and strategies leads to flexibility in solving problems. One method may be better suited to a particular problem.
3. Students learn that algorithms are "made objects" that can be compared, analyzed, and critiqued according to a number of criteria.

As the NCTM's Principles and Standards for School Mathematics (2000) states:

> "Having access to more than one method for each operation allows students to choose an approach that best fits the numbers in a particular problem." (page 155)

In students' study of calculation methods for each operation, they first build strategies with which they are comfortable, that make sense to them, that they can use fluently, and that they can gradually apply to harder problems. At a later time, they study some of the strategies with which they are less comfortable in order to learn about the mathematical relationships underlying them. This later period includes a study of conventional algorithms that are commonly used in students' communities. This study of conventional algorithms has both a mathematical and a social purpose.

First, students with good understanding of an operation—why it is used, what its properties are, how to use it efficiently, how it is related to other operations, and how the base-ten number system is used in that operation—can study an algorithm to delve further into the operation itself. Studying how and why an unfamiliar algorithm works challenges us to think through what we know about an operation. It requires pulling apart an algorithm, bringing meaning to shortcut notations, and finding parts of the algorithm that are similar to parts of more familiar algorithms.

For example, one of the authors noticed an older relative using the following algorithm to solve subtraction problems.

$$\begin{array}{r} 7_15 \\ -_439 \\ \hline 36 \end{array}$$

This woman had been educated in the United States in the early part of the 20th century, when this algorithm had been standard in some places in the country. By thinking through what this shortcut notation means, we can see that adding 10 to each number in the original problem, $(70 + 5) - (30 + 9)$, gives us an equivalent problem, $(70 + 15) - (40 + 9)$, that can be solved by subtracting each place. The underlying principle is that changing the two numbers in a subtraction problem by adding (or subtracting) the same amount results in a problem with the same answer as the original problem. Thinking through why an algorithm works brings us back to fundamental ideas about the operations—ideas on which these algorithms are based.

A second mathematical reason for studying the algorithms is that they have been found to be useful by many people. Too often, in the past, these algorithms were taught and learned without meaning. And, too often, these algorithms were seen as the central teaching tool for learning about an operation: learning addition was defined as learning the steps of the "carrying" algorithm. However, although the "carrying" algorithm may have held an inappropriately central place in our teaching strategies at one time, it is a perfectly good algorithm that can be used by those who find it useful. Competent adults often use different algorithms for different contexts, use a mixture of algorithms, or use one algorithm or strategy to check another. For example, one of the authors has a particular algorithm for subtraction that she uses only in her checkbook (it is neither the standard borrowing algorithm nor any of those used in this curriculum)—it is one that she has shaped to fit her particular needs in that context. So, a second reason for studying the conventional algorithms is to expose students to these algorithms and their underlying meaning. Those who find them sensible and useful may choose to adopt them for their own uses in life.

The third reason for studying conventional algorithms is that they are part of the social knowledge in students' communities. Adults in students' lives may use these algorithms, and they need not be a mystery to students. A variety of algorithms have been taught in different countries and at different times in the U.S. (e.g., the subtraction algorithm shown above). We recommend that you have students bring in algorithms used by adults in their families. You may find that there is more than one algorithm commonly used in your students' community for a particular operation.

There are two primary goals for the study of number and operations in the elementary grades.

a. Understanding the meaning and properties of the operations

b. Attaining computational fluency with whole numbers

It is these goals that underlie the choices we make in the study of algorithms and strategies. As stated in NCTM's *Principles and Standards:*

> "Students should come to view algorithms as tools for solving problems rather than as the goal of mathematics study. As students develop computational algorithms, teachers should evaluate their work, help them recognize efficient algorithms, and provide sufficient and appropriate practice so that they become fluent and flexible in computing."

Kilpatrick, Jeremy, Swafford, Jane, & Findell, Bradford (Eds.). (2001). *Adding It Up: Helping Children Learn Mathematics.* Washington, D.C.: National Academy Press.

National Council of Teachers of Mathematics (2000). *Principles and Standards for School Mathematics.* Reston, VA: NCTM.

Learning and Assessing Division Facts Related to Multiplication Combinations to 12 × 12

To develop efficient computation strategies, students need to become fluent with the multiplication combinations to 12 × 12 and the related division problems (e.g., 64 ÷ 8, 54 ÷ 6). Fluency with multiplication combinations and related division facts means that these are quickly accessible mentally, either because they are immediately known or because the calculation that is used is so effortless as to be essentially automatic. In *Investigations,* all students should be fluent with all of the multiplication combinations to 12 × 12 by the middle of Grade 4. They continue to practice and review these throughout Grade 4 and at the beginning of Grade 5. In Grade 5, students are expected to become fluent with the division problems that are related to these multiplication combinations. In referring to these related division problems, which cannot accurately be called *combinations,* it is often easier and more readily understandable to refer to them as *facts.*

The *Investigations* curriculum supports the importance of students' learning the basic facts fluently through a focus on reasoning about number relationships. Relying on memory alone is not sufficient, as many of us know from our own schooling. If you forget—as we all do at times— you are left with nothing. If, on the other hand, your learning is based on understanding of numbers and their relationships, you have a way to rethink and restructure your knowledge when you do not remember something.

Students use their understanding of the inverse relationship between multiplication and division to learn and then remember the division facts. For example, here is a set of linked multiplication and division equations:

$$8 \times 3 = 24 \qquad 3 \times 8 = 24$$

$$24 \div 8 = 3 \qquad 24 \div 3 = 8$$

The multiplication equations show the multiplication of two factors to equal a product. The division equations show that product divided by one of the factors to equal the other factor. When students are fluent with the factor pairs and their products that make up the multiplication combinations to 12 × 12, they use this knowledge to quickly access the answers to related division problems. For example, a student might say, "I know that 8 and 3 are factors that make 24, so when I see 24 divided by either 8 or 3, I have one factor and then I can think of what the other factor is."

In this unit, students review division facts as part of their ongoing practice of multiplication and division. They are assessed on division facts in Session 3.1, with the goal that all students become fluent with these division problems by the end of this unit. For this assessment, students are expected to be able to solve 30 problems that are representative of the set of division facts with accuracy in about 2 minutes. The reason for this is that it is assumed that in a short amount of time, students are either accessing these problems from memory or they are able to make a very quick calculation that is almost automatic. Some students may take longer than others to reach this level of fluency. You can expect to have students in your class who may need to do this assessment more than once, continuing to identify problems that they still need to work on and practice. You may need to provide additional practice, similar to the practice pages provided in the *Student Activity Book,* during this unit and after this unit is completed in order for some students to meet the goal of fluency.

Teacher Note

Assessment: Subtraction Problems

Problems 1 and 2

Benchmark addressed:

Benchmark 2: Solve subtraction problems accurately and efficiently, choosing from a variety of strategies.

Students have been studying and practicing different subtraction strategies and solving problems.

In order to meet the benchmark, students' work should show that they can:

- Break each problem into manageable pieces;

- Solve each piece accurately;

- Keep track of steps and determine the correct answer;

- Use clear and concise notation.

The following describes each of the two assessment problems and provides information on interpreting student work:

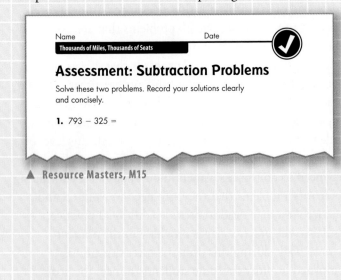

▲ **Resource Masters, M15**

Meeting the Benchmark

These students solved the problem accurately and efficiently by breaking the numbers apart in a variety of ways in order to do the subtraction. Students who add up, using efficient chunks of numbers, also meet the benchmark.

Charles broke apart 325 into 320 + 3 + 2. By looking at the numbers, he realizes that he can subtract 320 from 793 mentally. He knows that there is 5 more to subtract, and he subtracts it in two convenient parts.

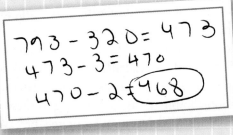

Charles' Work

Talisha breaks 325 apart by place, 300 + 20 + 5. Talisha uses a number line to subtract 5, then 20, and then 300. She understands that her jumps on the number line represent the amount she is subtracting and that 468, where she "lands," is her answer.

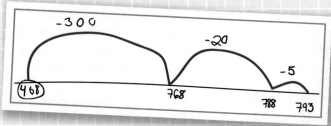

Talisha's Work

Olivia uses an expanded version of the U.S. algorithm to solve this problem. She breaks both numbers apart by place and then changes 90 + 3 to 80 + 13 so that she can subtract and get positive results.

Samantha also solves the problem by adding up and shows good number sense by first adding 75 to 325 to get to 400 and then adding 393 to reach 793. Samantha also understands that she needs to add 393 to 75 to get her answer, but she adds incorrectly.

Olivia's Work

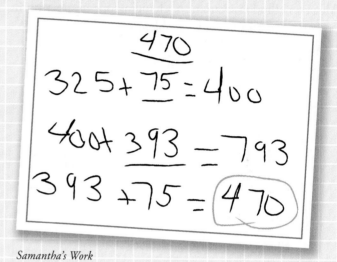

Samantha's Work

Partially Meeting the Benchmark

Some Grade 5 students understand subtraction and can solve the problem but are not yet efficient. Others use strategies efficiently but make small computational errors.

Renaldo solves the problem by adding up, but adds up by 100 at a time, and then 40, 20 and 8. To find how much he adds up, Renaldo also continues to add each 100 separately. Renaldo should be encouraged to add the largest "chunks" possible (in this case 325 + 400) to be more efficient.

Look at the work of students like Samantha on Problem 1, and use your knowledge of their work throughout this unit to determine whether these students generally subtract accurately or make frequent errors. Do they need to develop the habit of checking their work by using another strategy? Do they know their subtraction "facts"? Can they use what they know about subtraction with numbers less than 20 to add or subtract multiples of 10 and 100 (e.g., $7 - 3 = 4$, $70 - 30 = 40$, $700 - 300 = 400$)? Do they look carefully at the numbers to see whether their answer is sensible? For example, ask Samantha whether the difference between 793 and 325 could end in 0.

Renaldo's Work

Alicia explained her strategy this way: "I thought of 793 in two parts—700 and 93. And I thought of 325 in two parts—300 and 25. I made the 93 into 100 and subtracted 25 from it. That's 75. Then I subtracted 300 from 700. So far I had 400 + 75. But then I had to add on the extra 7." Alicia's method is a variant of changing one number in the problem. She thinks of the problem as $800 - 325 = 475$. However, instead of subtracting 7 from 475 to get the correct answer, she adds 7 to 475.

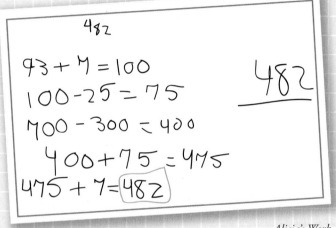

Alicia's Work

Help students like Alicia use a story context or number line to think through how she has changed the problem and how she must adjust the answer to find the difference to the original problem. It would also be important to know whether Alicia has another strategy she can use efficiently and accurately. If so, encourage her to continue to think through this new strategy by using a representation or story and to use another strategy to double-check her work.

Not Meeting the Benchmark

Some students may not yet have a solid understanding of subtraction. They may attempt to carry out strategies without meaning, losing track of what problem they are trying to solve or of the steps in their solution. These students may also make large computational errors.

Alex incorrectly subtracts 300 from 793. Although this is possibly a minor computation error, Alex should recognize that his answer is not reasonable. Subtracting 325 from a number less than 800 could not result in a difference greater than 500. He does subtract 25 correctly to get 568. Alex also strings his computation together, showing that he does not understand the use of the equal sign.

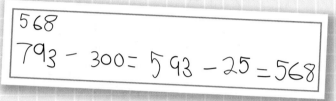

Alex's Work

Alex should be asked to solve the problem again to see whether he can reach the correct answer by using a different strategy. He also may benefit from solving more related problems similar to the ones on *Student Activity Book* pages 13 and 14. These problems are designed to help students use landmark numbers to help them subtract.

▲ **Resource Masters, M15**

Meeting the Benchmark

These students solve the problem accurately and efficiently, either subtracting by place or adding up by using efficient chunks of numbers.

Tavon breaks 510 apart and subtracts the parts. He breaks 510 into 100 and 410, subtracting first to get 12,000, and then subtracting 410.

11,590

$$12,100 - 100 = 12,000$$
$$12,000 - 410 = 11,590$$

Tavon's Work

Benito also breaks 510 apart and subtracts the parts. He breaks 510 into 500 and 10.

$$12,100 - 500 = 11,600$$

$$11,600 - 10 = 11,590$$

Benito's Work

Lourdes correctly uses the U.S. algorithm to solve this problem, subtracting each place, regrouping as necessary, and correctly notating her steps.

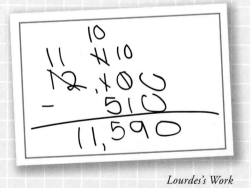

Lourdes's Work

Joshua uses an algorithm often seen in fifth-grade classrooms that involves negative numbers. He subtracts by place, noting whether each difference is positive or negative. He then combines his partial differences.

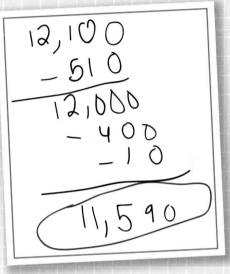

Joshua's Work

Tamira adds up to find her answer. She knows that $490 + 510 = 1,000$, adds 100 more to get 1,100 (because the total is 12,100), and then adds 11,000. She then combines her partial sums, which she has circled to help her keep track. This strategy is often done mentally, and it takes longer to write out the solution on an assessment than to solve the problem.

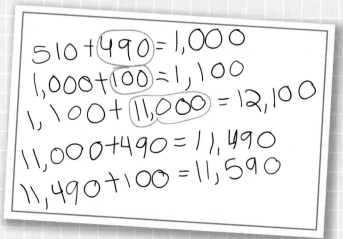

$$510 + 490 = 1,000$$
$$1,000 + 100 = 1,100$$
$$1,100 + 11,000 = 12,100$$
$$11,000 + 490 = 11,490$$
$$11,490 + 100 = 11,590$$

Tamira's Work

Partially Meeting the Benchmark

Some fifth graders understand subtraction and can solve the problem but are not yet efficient. Others use strategies efficiently but make small computational errors.

Shandra gets the correct answer by adding up on a number line, and her jumps utilize multiples of 100; yet she could be more efficient in those jumps. It is not clear without asking her why her first jump was of 500 (to 1,010). When she gets to 1,100, she does not recognize that the difference between 1,100 and 12,100 is a multiple of 1,000, and instead she adds on 900 + 10,000 + 100. Shandra needs to practice adding up by using larger "chunks."

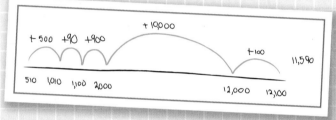

Shandra's Work

Other students only partially meet the benchmark if they break the numbers apart in inefficient ways or if they make minor computation errors in their solutions. Students who break the numbers in inefficient ways should be asked to solve the problem by using fewer steps. This may encourage some students to combine steps or use larger, more efficient groups. Students who make minor computation errors should be asked to solve the problem again to see whether they can correct their errors on their own.

Not Meeting the Benchmark

Some students may not yet have a solid understanding of subtraction. They may confuse strategies, lose track of what problem they are trying to solve, or make large computational errors.

Zachary attempts to use a number line and subtract back from 12,100 to 510. He makes two mistakes in his second jump from 12,000 to 1,000, recording 1,200, which appears to be both a computation error and a place-value

error. Zachary also does not show what his answer is, making no attempt to combine his partial differences.

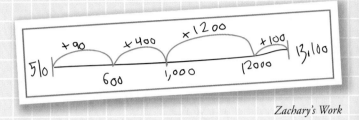

Zachary's Work

Students who do not meet the benchmark need to continue to practice whichever strategy is most accessible to them, which may be to subtract in parts, usually by place. Continue to model whichever strategy you and the student choose and provide opportunities to practice it. When students gain proficiency with their chosen strategies, suggest that they try variations, such as finding different (and more efficient) ways to break the numbers apart. These students may benefit from solving more related problems similar to the ones on *Student Activity Book* pages 13 and 14. These problems are designed to help students use landmark numbers to help them subtract.

Looking at Both Problems

You can also use this assessment as an opportunity to look at your students' flexibility with subtraction. These problems have different characteristics, the sizes of the numbers are different, and Problem 2 involves numbers that are both multiples of 100.

- Do students use the same strategy for both problems? Are they using the strategy efficiently?

- Do students recognize that quickly looking at the numbers first might help them choose what strategy they should use?

As they continue work in this unit, encourage all students to try different strategies so that they are flexible and fluent in solving subtraction problems.

Teacher Note

End-of-Unit Assessment

Problem 1

Benchmark addressed:

Benchmark 2: Solve subtraction problems accurately and efficiently, choosing from a variety of strategies.

In order to meet the benchmark, students' work should show that they can:

- Break each problem into manageable pieces;

- Solve each piece accurately;

- Keep track of steps and determine the correct answer;

- Use clear and concise notation.

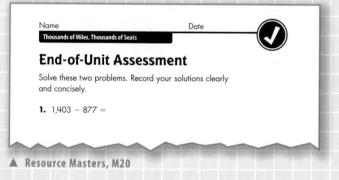

Name _____ Date _____ ✓

Thousands of Miles, Thousands of Seats

End-of-Unit Assessment

Solve these two problems. Record your solutions clearly and concisely.

1. 1,403 − 877 =

▲ Resource Masters, M20

Meeting the Benchmark

These students solve the problem accurately and efficiently, either by subtracting by place, or adding up using efficient chunks of numbers. Students who subtract back efficiently also meet the benchmark.

Hana breaks 877 apart by place, correctly subtracting 800, 70, and 7.

Hana's Work

Tyler adds up. He first adds 877 + 123 and gets 1,000. From playing *Close to 1,000* and from other place-value work, many students easily know these "combinations" of 1,000. He then knows it is 403 more to 1,403. Tyler then combines his partial sums correctly.

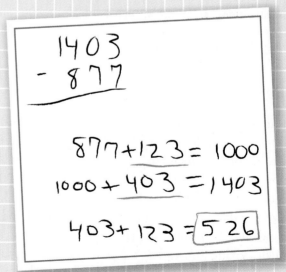

Tyler's Work

Professional Development: Teacher Notes **137**

Partially Meeting the Benchmark

These students understand subtraction and have a strategy to use, but they either use the strategy inefficiently or make minor computation errors.

Martin uses the U.S. standard algorithm for subtraction, and makes a very common error when zero is involved or when regrouping is needed in more than one place. He correctly regroups the 10s and 100s so that he has ten 10s in the tens place, but he does not regroup the tens and ones correctly. Instead, he simply creates 13 in the ones place without decreasing the tens by one. He has, in effect, added 10 to 1,403: $1,300 + 100 + 13 = 1,413$. Therefore, his solution is ten more than the correct answer.

Martin's Work

Some students may make minor computation errors, such as Martin. Other students may arrive at the correct answer, but use strategies inefficiently, such as breaking 800 into smaller numbers. Fifth-grade students should be able to mentally solve $1,403 - 800$.

Not Meeting the Benchmark

Avery attempts to use an expanded version of the U.S. algorithm by breaking 1,403 into $1,000 + 400 + 00 + 3$. At first, he correctly regroups in the hundreds and tens place by subtracting 100 from 400 and adding that 100 to the tens place, resulting in $1,000 + 300 + 100 + 3$. However, he then subtracts another 100 from the hundreds place and adds 10 to the ones place, as if these were equivalent, giving him $1,000 + 200 + 100 + 13$. Finally, he correctly adds 1,000 to the 200 in the hundreds place to

get $1,200 + 100 + 13$ and subtracts. His answer is 90 less than the correct answer because of the step in which he subtracted 100 from 300, but added only 10 to the 3 in the ones place. Avery is also not looking at his result to see whether he has a reasonable answer: subtracting a little less than 900 from about 1,400 should result in an answer a little more than 500.

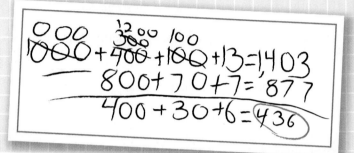

Avery's Work

Students who make large computational errors or use strategies incorrectly because they don't understand them also do not meet the benchmark. These students should focus on picking one strategy they can use with understanding and continue practice using it.

Problem 2

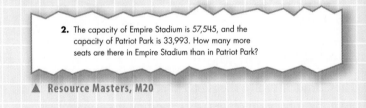

2. The capacity of Empire Stadium is 57,545, and the capacity of Patriot Park is 33,993. How many more seats are there in Empire Stadium than in Patriot Park?

▲ **Resource Masters, M20**

Meeting the Benchmark

These students solve the problem accurately and efficiently, either subtracting by place or taking advantage of how close 33,993 is to 34,000.

Terrence breaks 57,545 apart by place, and then regroups in the 1,000s, 100s, and 10s places, so that he can subtract easily in each place.

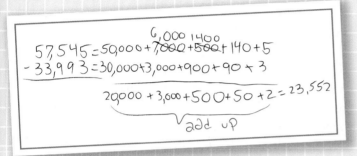

Terrence's Work

Cecilia uses the U.S. standard algorithm correctly.

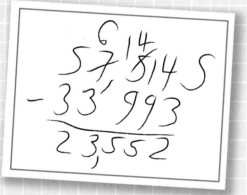

Cecilia's Work

Rachel adds up mentally to find her answer. She recognizes 33,993 is close to 34,000, a "landmark" number, and adds 7. She continues to add up and is able to do this in only one step, adding 23,545 to reach 57,545. She combines her partial sums (7 and 23,545) to reach her final answer.

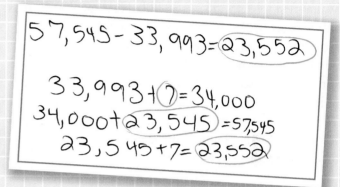

Rachel's Work

Like Rachel, Mitch recognizes 34,000 is easier to work with and uses it to solve 57,545 − 34,000. Because he has subtracted 7 too many, he adds 7 to get the correct answer.

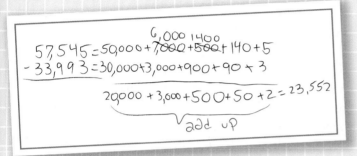

Mitch's Work

Partially Meeting the Benchmark

Some fifth graders understand subtraction and can solve the problem, but are not yet efficient. Others use strategies efficiently, but make small computational errors.

Walter first solves 57,545 − 30,000. He recognizes he must still subtract 3,993 and uses the U.S. standard algorithm. He regroups correctly, but when he solves 14 − 9 (in the hundreds place) he writes 7. The teacher needs to check with Walter to see if this is only a minor computation error or if Walter is having trouble reading his own notation. The lack of clarity in the notation makes it difficult to see whether Walter found it difficult to keep track of regrouping across several places.

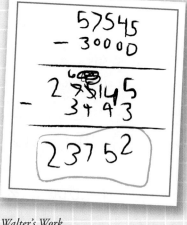

Walter's Work

Nora starts by solving 57,545 − 33,000 correctly. She knows she still has to subtract 993, which she breaks apart into 990 and 3. When she solves 24,545 − 990, she gets 23,595, which is incorrect. Since it is not clear from her work how she arrives at this answer, the teacher needs to ask her about her work.

$$57,545 - 33,993 =$$
$$57,545 - 33,000 = 24,545$$
$$24,545 - 990 = 23595 \leftarrow$$
$$23,595 - 3 = \boxed{23592}$$

Nora's Work

For some students, subtracting 990 from 24,545 is too much of a challenge. These students may need practice subtracting multiples of 10, 100, and 1,000. Provide more opportunities to solve problems such as: 24,595 − 100, 24,585 − 500, 24,595 − 550, and so on. (See the problems in Session 1.4).

Janet uses a version of a number line and adds up from 33,993 to 57,545. She gets the correct answer by adding up her partial sums. However, Janet could be more efficient with her strategy. While she uses landmark numbers, adding to 34,000, then 40,000, then 50,000, then 57,000, and finally 57,545, she needs to work on greater efficiency in combining steps, either completing the problem with one step, as Rachel did, or using fewer steps.

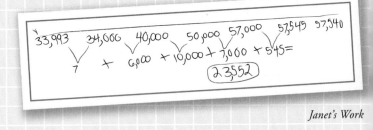

Janet's Work

Not Meeting the Benchmark

Some students may not yet have a solid understanding of subtraction, and they may confuse strategies, lose track of what problem they are trying to solve, or make large computational errors.

Margaret uses a number line and efficiently adds up to 34,000, 57,000, and 57,545. However, for the jump between 34,000 and 57,000 she writes "23", which is the number of thousands. She correctly combines 545 + 23 + 7, but seems unaware that this answer makes no sense. Margaret has lost sight of the magnitude of the numbers in the problem.

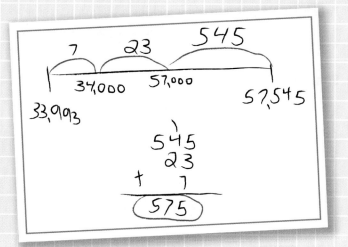

Margaret's Work

Felix starts to subtract 33,993 in parts by correctly subtracting 33,000 from 57,545. He then appears to abandon this strategy and starts over again by subtracting 33,000 from 57,000, again correctly. In order to complete this strategy, he attempts to subtract 545 − 993, which, if done correctly, would work. It may be that Felix has seen other students in the class subtract by place, then combine the results, some of which are positive and some of which are negative. (See **Teacher Note:** Subtraction Strategies on page 119.) However, he is unable to carry this out correctly. In the ones place, he subtracts 5 − 3; in the tens place he subtracts 9 − 4; and in the hundreds place he probably subtracts 9 − 5, but writes down an incorrect difference of 5.

$$57545 - 33000 = 24545 \qquad 57000 - 33000 = 24000$$
$$545 - 993 = -552$$
$$27000 - 552 = \boxed{23448}$$

Felix's Work

Students who do not meet the benchmark should continue to practice whichever strategy is most accessible to them, which may be to subtract one number in parts, usually by place. Continue to model whichever strategy you and the students choose and provide opportunities to practice it. Once students gain proficiency with their chosen strategies, suggest that they try variations, such as finding different (and more efficient) ways to break the numbers apart.

Dialogue Box

How Many Steps to 10,000?

The students in this Grade 5 class were introduced to the 10,000 chart in Session 1.1. Using the chart, they explored the structure of the number 10,000, labeled useful landmark numbers, and, starting with a given number, added or subtracted multiples of 100. Today they are finding the difference between a given number and 10,000. The teacher asks them first to locate 1,025 on the chart and then to find the number of steps on the chart from 1,025 to 10,000. She gives them a few minutes to work on the problem and then asks them to share solutions. She specifically asks certain students to share and wants to highlight different ways solutions can be notated.

Teacher: I've asked some students to explain the strategy they used to find out how many steps it is from 1,025 to 10,000. Remember that our imaginary creature starts at 1,025 and takes one step on every square, so the first step is onto square 1,026, the next onto 1,027, and so on up to 10,000. How many steps would it have to take? Shandra?

Shandra: I used a number line because it's easier for me. First I jumped 8,000, and that got me to 9,025; then I went 900 more, and that was 9,925. I needed 75 more to get to 10,000 on the chart.

Shandra draws the following on the board:

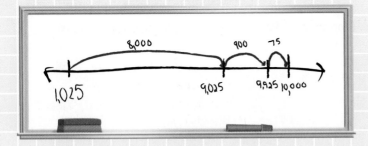

As Shandra is explaining her number line, the teacher writes these equations on the board:

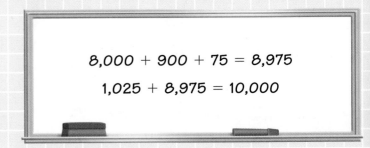

$$1,025 + 8,000 = 9,025$$
$$9,025 + 900 = 9,925$$
$$9,925 + 75 = 10,000$$

Teacher: So you started by making a big jump, trying to get as close to 10,000 as possible. Are you finished? What did you do to find out the answer?

Shandra: You add 8,000, 900, and 75, and that's 8,975.

The teacher adds the following equations to the board:

$$8,000 + 900 + 75 = 8,975$$
$$1,025 + 8,975 = 10,000$$

Teacher: So here's one way to get to 10,000. Stuart solved the problem another way. Stuart?

Stuart: I wanted to get to a landmark, so I added 75 to 1,025. I added 400 more to get me to another landmark. I know that 85 + 15 = 100, so 8,500 + 1,500 will equal 10,000.

As Stuart explains his solution, he writes the following on the board:

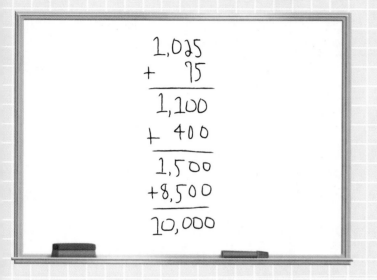

Teacher: What do you do next?

Stuart: I added 75, 400, and 8,500. That's easy. 400 + 75 is 475, and 8,500 + 475 = 8,975.

Stuart adds the following to the board:

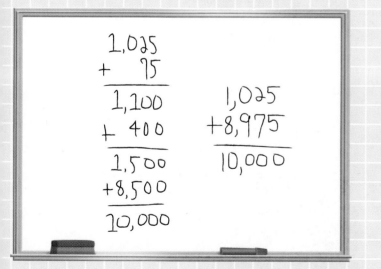

Teacher: Stuart wanted to get to landmark numbers first. Instead of making a big jump first, he went to a near landmark, a multiple of 100. I noticed that Charles used the 10,000 chart to help him. Charles?

Charles: I started at 10,000 and went back to 2,000. Then I went 9 rows up the chart to 1,100. Then I knew it was 75 more back to 1,025.

While Charles is demonstrating his moves on the 10,000 chart, the teacher writes the following on the board:

$$10,000 - 8,000 = 2,000$$
$$2,000 - 900 = 1,100$$
$$1,100 - 75 = 1,025$$

Teacher: How did you keep track of the moves you made from 10,000 to 1,025?

Charles: I know that I went 8,000 to get to 2,000 because I know 10,000 − 2,000 = 8,000. 9 rows up is 900 because each row is 100. And I know 100 − 75 is 25, so I landed on 1,025.

The teacher writes the following on the board:

$$8,000 + 900 + 75 = 8,975$$
$$10,000 - 8,975 = 1,025$$

Teacher: I want you to look at something and think about it for a minute. [Circles Shandra's number line and Charles's equations on the board] How are these the same? How are they different?

Hana: They both used the same numbers. Charles added the same numbers that Shandra did, but he did it backward. He minused from 10,000, but she added from 1,025.

Teacher: You're right. Does it matter which way you go?

Hana: No, because the space between them is the same. In the end you add the same numbers.

Teacher: That's right. Even though Shandra added up from 1,025 and Charles subtracted down from 10,000, they both found the difference between 1,025 and 10,000.

The solutions above show different ways that students find the difference between 1,025 and 10,000. As the teacher observes students, she looks for specific strategies and notations she wants other students in the classroom to see —how Shandra uses a number line, the way Stuart uses vertical notation in his work, and how Charles subtracts to find the answer. Throughout this unit, students are encouraged to think through and use a variety of strategies efficiently. The teacher records these strategies to model examples of clear and concise notation.

Dialogue Box

Classifying and Naming Subtraction Strategies

The students in this Grade 5 class are reviewing subtraction, which they studied in-depth in Grade 4. In Session 2.1, they are solving the problem 892 − 567. They explain the strategies they used to solve this problem and classify them on the basis of how each solution starts.

Teacher: Let's hear some strategies. You are going to explain how you solved the problem and what your answer is. We're going to hear some different ways to solve 892 − 567.

Joshua: I used the number line. I started with 892 and wanted to get to 567. First I subtracted 92. That's 800, which is a tens number. Then I subtracted 200 more and it gave me 600. 600 − 30 = 570 and minus 3 more is 567.

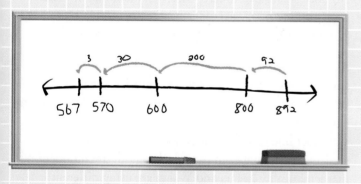

Teacher: So what is your answer?

Joshua: I added 92 + 200 + 30 + 3 and it's 325.

Nora: I did a different number line strategy. I put the 567 on and the 892 on and I hopped between the numbers, from 567 to 600, then to 800 and 892. I added 33 to get to 600, then 200, and then 92. When I added them all up I got 325, too.

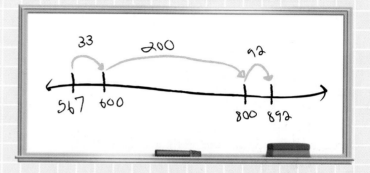

Yumiko: We should call them the "number line strategy."

Teacher: Nora and Joshua are both using the number line to help them find the difference between 567 and 892. Do we want to say that it's the same strategy? The way they're getting there is very important.

Yumiko: Joshua started at 892 and subtracted, but Nora added. Nora is adding up on the number line. I think we should call it "adding up."

Teacher: So Nora found the difference by adding, and Yumiko thinks we should call it "adding up." What did Joshua do?

Yumiko: He jumped back 92 and went to a tens number. Then he minused more until he got to 567. He subtracted on the number line. Maybe we could call it "subtracting down"?

Teacher: Joshua subtracted on the number line until he got to 567. They both found the distance between the two numbers on the number line, but in a different way. I think the names "adding up" and "subtracting down" really capture how they are different.

The teacher writes the strategies on different charts.

Walter: I used the number line too, but it's different. The problem was 892 − 567. I put the 892 on first and hopped back 500, then 60, and then 7 more. That took me to 325, and that's my answer.

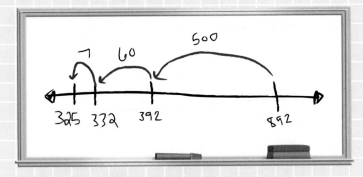

Teacher: Lourdes, you used the number line, but you subtracted 567 as you moved down the number line. Instead of jumping to 567, you subtracted 567 in chunks.

Lourdes: I also minused from 892, but I broke it (567) up differently. I subtracted 2 to get 890, then 60 to get 830, then 500 to get 330 and then I still had 5 left to subtract, so it was 325.

The teacher records Lourdes' work on the board:

$$
\begin{array}{r}
892 \\
-\ 2 \\
\hline
890 \\
-\ 60 \\
\hline
830 \\
-\ 500 \\
\hline
330 \\
-\ 5 \\
\hline
325
\end{array}
$$

Teacher: You both took the second number and split it into parts. You subtracted in parts. I've heard some of you call this strategy "subtracting the second number in parts."

The teacher adds another heading on the poster and writes Walter's and Lourdes's strategies under it.

Teacher: Does anyone else have a different strategy?

Zachary: I changed 892 to 897 by adding 5. It's easier to take away if you start with 897. Then 897 − 567 = 330. Then the 5 I added to 892, I removed from 330 to change it back and it gave me 325.

The teacher writes the following on the board:

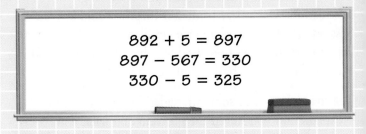

Teacher: What Zachary did is change the first number to make the digits in the tens and ones place the same as in the second number. Then at the end, he adjusted the answer by subtracting 5. We'll call this "changing one number and adjusting." You can use this strategy in many ways. Did anyone else use this type of strategy?

No one else seemed to have used this method, and some students look perplexed. The teacher knows that there will be an opportunity to discuss this strategy further in Session 2.3.

As the teacher asks the students to decide what is the same and what is different about these strategies, she is listening for an understanding of the general approach taken by each student. This teacher notices a number of students using a number line to solve subtraction problems. She wants students to see that even though they both use number lines, mathematically, Joshua and Walter are using different, although related, subtraction strategies. She also wants the students to notice that, although Walter and Lourdes broke 567 apart in different ways, they were using the same basic subtraction strategy. In some classes, students name the strategy for the person who shared the strategy (i.e., "Walter's strategy"). Although personalizing the strategy has its merits, it is beneficial to name the strategy by the general way the problem is started so that the mathematical approach is emphasized. Naming strategies and keeping them posted provides students with some language to describe their subtraction strategies and raises students' awareness of approaches to consider when they are solving problems.

Working with the U.S. Algorithm

During the past few days, students in this Grade 5 class have been sharing, exploring, and using various subtraction strategies. One of the strategies that several students use is the U.S. algorithm. In this session, students study this strategy, trying to understand its notation. The class has already looked at one example, $674 - 328$, in which one ten is "borrowed." Now they look at a more difficult problem.

$$463$$
$$- 279$$

Teacher: We're going to solve this next problem by looking carefully at what happens in each place. Can someone come up and rewrite the numbers by place value?

Martin comes up to the board and rewrites the problem:

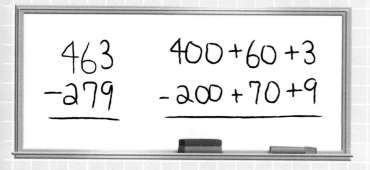

The teacher adds parentheses to what Martin wrote on the board:

Teacher: I wrote the parentheses to show that we are subtracting all the parts of the bottom number. Let's try to solve this problem, the way they do in the U.S. algorithm. Martin, what's the first thing you're going to do?

Martin: I start in the ones place. If I subtract 9 from 3, I get a negative number, so I have to trade for a 10. Wait a minute, I have to trade for a 100! You need to take 100 from the 400 and add that 100 to the 60. Then take a 10 from the 160 and add it to the 3. That will make the 160 a 150.

The teacher adds to what Martin wrote on the board:

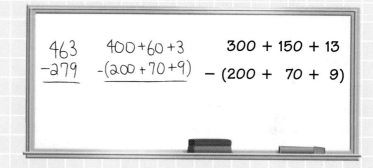

Teacher: Is that what you mean?

Martin: Yes.

Teacher: Let's slow down a minute because Martin combined two steps. Martin, you started to trade for a 10 and then said you had to trade for a 100. Why?

Martin: When I looked at the 60, I realized that I couldn't subtract the tens either without getting a negative number, so I just got a 100 and gave it to the 60.

Teacher: Good. So what should the top numbers add up to?

Lourdes: 463.

Teacher: Who can finish the problem?

Hana: 300 − 200 is 100, 150 − 70 is 80, and 13 − 9 is 4. I add them all up and it's . . . 184.

The teacher adds Hana's responses to the problems on the board:

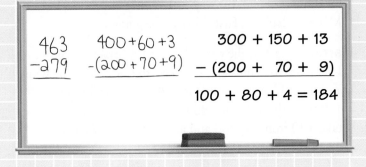

Teacher: What we did is separate the numbers to show how the algorithm works, but when people use the actual algorithm, they don't write out all the numbers. Let's see what that looks like. Tavon, you use this strategy often. Can you show us, using this problem?

Tavon: 3 take away 9 and I can't do that, I mean it's a negative, so I cross out the 6 tens and make it a 5 and then make that a 13. 13 minus 9 is 4. Then 5 − 7, I can't do that, so I cross out the 4 and make it a 3 and 15 minus 7 is 8.

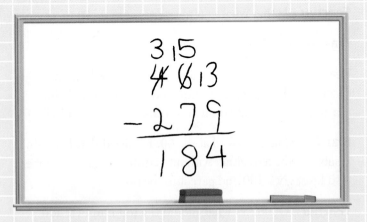

Teacher: Hold on a second. Let's go over that. Where did you get that little 1 you put next to the 3 and what does that mean?

Tavon: When I crossed out the 6 and made it 5, I was taking 1 ten. Then I added 1, I mean 10, to the 3, so I had 13.

Teacher: So you had 63, but you made it into 50 + 13, which is still 63. Then what?

Tavon: Then 5 minus 7, I can't do that either, so I cross out the 4 and make it a 3 and 15 minus 7 is 8.

Teacher: 15 is really 15 what?

Tavon: 15 tens.

Teacher: So you're subtracting 7 tens from 15 tens. Does everybody get that?

Tavon: All I have left is 3 minus 2 equals 1, I mean 100, so the answer's the same.

Teacher: So if we look at what Tavon did and what Martin did, we should see some similarities.

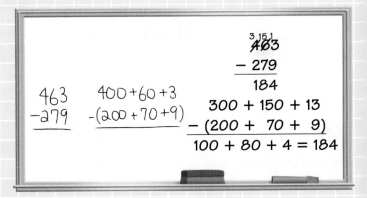

Teacher: Everyone is going to try a few problems with this algorithm and try to understand the notation. If you don't like it, that's fine. But just like you are learning about other strategies you may not use, learning about this one helps you continue to learn more about different ways to think about subtraction.

The teacher encourages students to practice different strategies and notation and also stresses that sense-making is vital.

Student Math Handbook

The *Student Math Handbook* pages related to this unit are pictured on the following pages. This book is designed to be used flexibly: as a resource for students doing classwork, as a book students can take home for reference while doing homework and playing math games with their families, and as a reference for families to better understand the work their children are doing in class.

When students take the *Student Math Handbook* home, they and their families can discuss these pages together to reinforce or enhance students' understanding of the mathematical concepts and games in this unit.

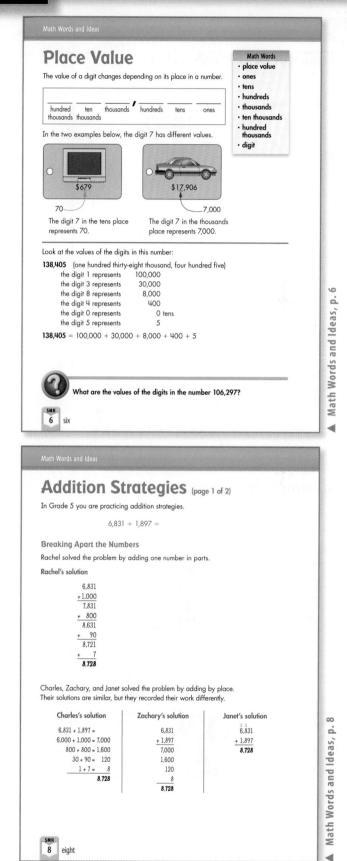

▲ Math Words and Ideas, p. 6

Math Words and Ideas

Place Value

The value of a digit changes depending on its place in a number.

Math Words
- place value
- ones
- tens
- hundreds
- thousands
- ten thousands
- hundred thousands
- digit

hundred thousands | ten thousands | thousands , hundreds | tens | ones

In the two examples below, the digit 7 has different values.

$679

The digit 7 in the tens place represents 70.

$17,906

The digit 7 in the thousands place represents 7,000.

Look at the values of the digits in this number:

138,405 (one hundred thirty-eight thousand, four hundred five)

the digit 1 represents	100,000
the digit 3 represents	30,000
the digit 8 represents	8,000
the digit 4 represents	400
the digit 0 represents	0 tens
the digit 5 represents	5

138,405 = 100,000 + 30,000 + 8,000 + 400 + 5

? What are the values of the digits in the number 106,297?

SMH **6** six

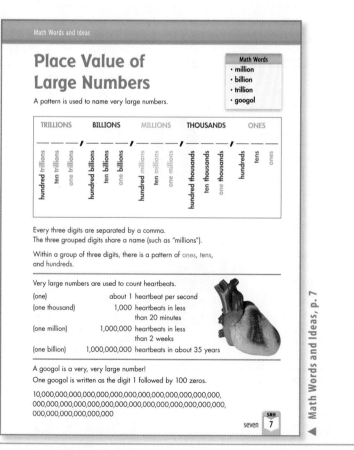

Math Words and Ideas

Place Value of Large Numbers

Math Words
- million
- billion
- trillion
- googol

A pattern is used to name very large numbers.

TRILLIONS	BILLIONS	MILLIONS	THOUSANDS	ONES
hundred trillions / ten trillions / one trillions	hundred billions / ten billions / one billions	hundred millions / ten millions / one millions	hundred thousands / ten thousands / one thousands	hundreds / tens / ones

Every three digits are separated by a comma.
The three grouped digits share a name (such as "millions").

Within a group of three digits, there is a pattern of ones, tens, and hundreds.

Very large numbers are used to count heartbeats.

(one)	about 1 heartbeat per second
(one thousand)	1,000 heartbeats in less than 20 minutes
(one million)	1,000,000 heartbeats in less than 2 weeks
(one billion)	1,000,000,000 heartbeats in about 35 years

A googol is a very, very large number!
One googol is written as the digit 1 followed by 100 zeros.

10,000,000,000,000,000,000,000,000,000,000,000,000,000,000,000,000,
000,000,000,000,000,000,000,000,000,000,000,000,000,000,000,000,000,
000,000,000,000,000,000

seven SMH **7**

▲ Math Words and Ideas, p. 7

Math Words and Ideas

Addition Strategies (page 1 of 2)

In Grade 5 you are practicing addition strategies.

6,831 + 1,897 =

Breaking Apart the Numbers

Rachel solved the problem by adding one number in parts.

Rachel's solution

```
    6,831
  + 1,000
    7,831
  +   800
    8,631
  +    90
    8,721
  +     7
    8,728
```

Charles, Zachary, and Janet solved the problem by adding by place. Their solutions are similar, but they recorded their work differently.

Charles's solution	Zachary's solution	Janet's solution
6,831 + 1,897 =	6,831	¹ ¹ 6,831
6,000 + 1,000 = 7,000	+ 1,897	+ 1,897
800 + 800 = 1,600	7,000	8,728
30 + 90 = 120	1,600	
1 + 7 = 8	120	
8,728	8	
	8,728	

SMH **8** eight

▲ Math Words and Ideas, p. 8

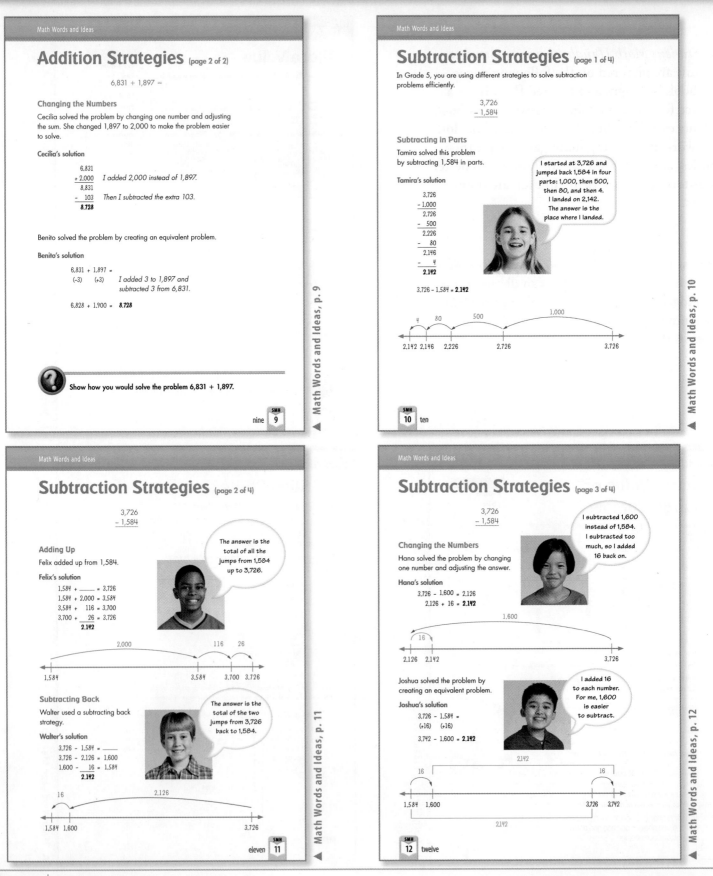

Panel 1 (top-left)

Math Words and Ideas

Addition Strategies (page 2 of 2)

6,831 + 1,897 =

Changing the Numbers

Cecilia solved the problem by changing one number and adjusting the sum. She changed 1,897 to 2,000 to make the problem easier to solve.

Cecilia's solution

```
    6,831
  + 2,000    I added 2,000 instead of 1,897.
    8,831
  -   103    Then I subtracted the extra 103.
    8,728
```

Benito solved the problem by creating an equivalent problem.

Benito's solution

```
  6,831 + 1,897 =
  (-3)    (+3)     I added 3 to 1,897 and
                   subtracted 3 from 6,831.
  6,828 + 1,900 = 8,728
```

? Show how you would solve the problem 6,831 + 1,897.

nine **9** SMH

◄ Math Words and Ideas, p. 9

Panel 2 (top-right)

Math Words and Ideas

Subtraction Strategies (page 1 of 4)

In Grade 5, you are using different strategies to solve subtraction problems efficiently.

```
   3,726
 - 1,584
```

Subtracting in Parts

Tamira solved this problem by subtracting 1,584 in parts.

Tamira's solution

```
   3,726
 - 1,000
   2,726
 -   500
   2,226
 -    80
   2,146
 -     4
   2,142
```

3,726 - 1,584 = **2,142**

> I started at 3,726 and jumped back 1,584 in four parts: 1,000, then 500, then 80, and then 4. I landed on 2,142. The answer is the place where I landed.

Number line: 2,142 2,146 2,226 2,726 3,726 with jumps 4, 80, 500, 1,000

SMH **10** ten

◄ Math Words and Ideas, p. 10

Panel 3 (bottom-left)

Math Words and Ideas

Subtraction Strategies (page 2 of 4)

```
   3,726
 - 1,584
```

Adding Up

Felix added up from 1,584.

Felix's solution

```
  1,584 + _____ = 3,726
  1,584 + 2,000 = 3,584
  3,584 +   116 = 3,700
  3,700 +    26 = 3,726
              2,142
```

> The answer is the total of all the jumps from 1,584 up to 3,726.

Number line: 1,584 3,584 3,700 3,726 with jumps 2,000, 116, 26

Subtracting Back

Walter used a subtracting back strategy.

Walter's solution

```
  3,726 - 1,584 = _____
  3,726 - 2,126 = 1,600
  1,600 -    16 = 1,584
            2,142
```

> The answer is the total of the two jumps from 3,726 back to 1,584.

Number line: 1,584 1,600 3,726 with jumps 16, 2,126

eleven **11** SMH

◄ Math Words and Ideas, p. 11

Panel 4 (bottom-right)

Math Words and Ideas

Subtraction Strategies (page 3 of 4)

```
   3,726
 - 1,584
```

Changing the Numbers

Hana solved the problem by changing one number and adjusting the answer.

Hana's solution

```
  3,726 - 1,600 = 2,126
  2,126 +    16 = 2,142
```

> I subtracted 1,600 instead of 1,584. I subtracted too much, so I added 16 back on.

Number line: 2,126 2,142 ... 3,726 with 16 and 1,600

Joshua solved the problem by creating an equivalent problem.

Joshua's solution

```
  3,726 - 1,584 =
  (+16)   (+16)
  3,742 - 1,600 = 2,142
```

> I added 16 to each number. For me, 1,600 is easier to subtract.

Number line: 1,584 1,600 ... 3,726 3,742 with 16, 2,142, 16

SMH **12** twelve

◄ Math Words and Ideas, p. 12

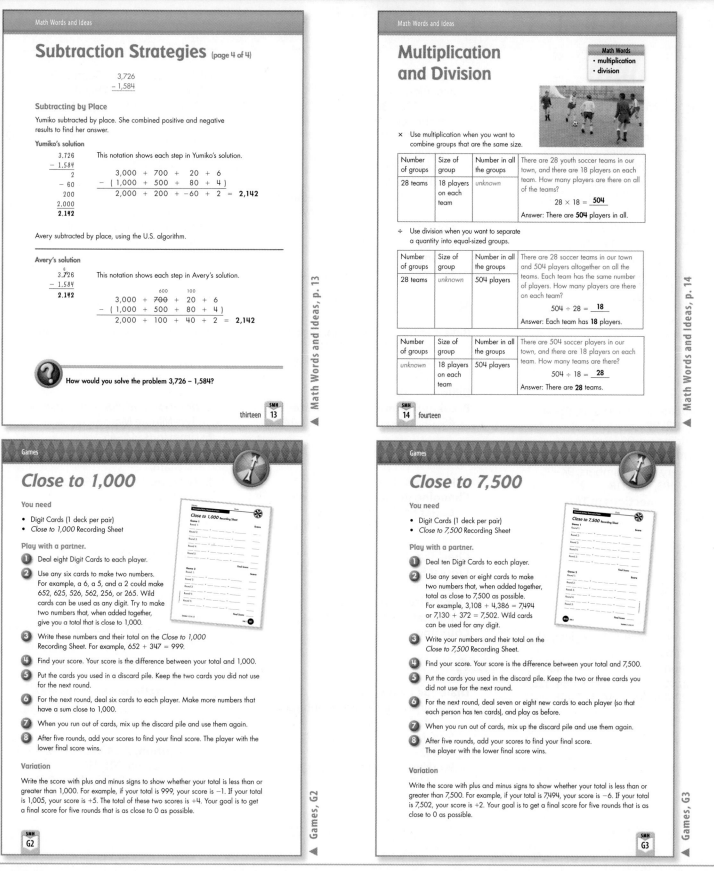

Math Words and Ideas

Subtraction Strategies (page 4 of 4)

$$3,726$$
$$- 1,584$$

Subtracting by Place

Yumiko subtracted by place. She combined positive and negative results to find her answer.

Yumiko's solution

$$
\begin{array}{r}
3,726 \\
- 1,584 \\
\hline
2 \\
-60 \\
200 \\
2,000 \\
\hline
\mathbf{2,142}
\end{array}
$$

This notation shows each step in Yumiko's solution.

$$
\begin{array}{c}
3,000 + 700 + 20 + 6 \\
- (1,000 + 500 + 80 + 4) \\
\hline
2,000 + 200 + -60 + 2 = \mathbf{2,142}
\end{array}
$$

Avery subtracted by place, using the U.S. algorithm.

Avery's solution

$$
\begin{array}{r}
\overset{6}{3,\cancel{7}26} \\
- 1,584 \\
\hline
\mathbf{2,142}
\end{array}
$$

This notation shows each step in Avery's solution.

$$
\begin{array}{c}
\quad\quad\quad\quad 600 \quad 100 \\
3,000 + \cancel{700} + 20 + 6 \\
- (1,000 + 500 + 80 + 4) \\
\hline
2,000 + 100 + 40 + 2 = \mathbf{2,142}
\end{array}
$$

? How would you solve the problem 3,726 – 1,584?

thirteen **SMH 13**

◄ Math Words and Ideas, p. 13

Math Words and Ideas

Multiplication and Division

Math Words
- multiplication
- division

× Use multiplication when you want to combine groups that are the same size.

Number of groups	Size of group	Number in all the groups	
28 teams	18 players on each team	*unknown*	There are 28 youth soccer teams in our town, and there are 18 players on each team. How many players are there on all of the teams? $28 \times 18 = \underline{504}$ Answer: There are **504** players in all.

÷ Use division when you want to separate a quantity into equal-sized groups.

Number of groups	Size of group	Number in all the groups	
28 teams	*unknown*	504 players	There are 28 soccer teams in our town and 504 players altogether on all the teams. Each team has the same number of players. How many players are there on each team? $504 \div 28 = \underline{18}$ Answer: Each team has **18** players.

Number of groups	Size of group	Number in all the groups	
unknown	18 players on each team	504 players	There are 504 soccer players in our town, and there are 18 players on each team. How many teams are there? $504 \div 18 = \underline{28}$ Answer: There are **28** teams.

SMH 14 fourteen

◄ Math Words and Ideas, p. 14

Games

Close to 1,000

You need
- Digit Cards (1 deck per pair)
- *Close to 1,000* Recording Sheet

Play with a partner.

1 Deal eight Digit Cards to each player.

2 Use any six cards to make two numbers. For example, a 6, a 5, and a 2 could make 652, 625, 526, 562, 256, or 265. Wild cards can be used as any digit. Try to make two numbers that, when added together, give you a total that is close to 1,000.

3 Write these numbers and their total on the *Close to 1,000* Recording Sheet. For example, 652 + 347 = 999.

4 Find your score. Your score is the difference between your total and 1,000.

5 Put the cards you used in a discard pile. Keep the two cards you did not use for the next round.

6 For the next round, deal six cards to each player. Make more numbers that have a sum close to 1,000.

7 When you run out of cards, mix up the discard pile and use them again.

8 After five rounds, add your scores to find your final score. The player with the lower final score wins.

Variation

Write the score with plus and minus signs to show whether your total is less than or greater than 1,000. For example, if your total is 999, your score is –1. If your total is 1,005, your score is +5. The total of these two scores is +4. Your goal is to get a final score for five rounds that is as close to 0 as possible.

SMH G2

◄ Games, G2

Games

Close to 7,500

You need
- Digit Cards (1 deck per pair)
- *Close to 7,500* Recording Sheet

Play with a partner.

1 Deal ten Digit Cards to each player.

2 Use any seven or eight cards to make two numbers that, when added together, total as close to 7,500 as possible. For example, 3,108 + 4,386 = 7,494 or 7,130 + 372 = 7,502. Wild cards can be used for any digit.

3 Write your numbers and their total on the *Close to 7,500* Recording Sheet.

4 Find your score. Your score is the difference between your total and 7,500.

5 Put the cards you used in the discard pile. Keep the two or three cards you did not use for the next round.

6 For the next round, deal seven or eight new cards to each player (so that each person has ten cards), and play as before.

7 When you run out of cards, mix up the discard pile and use them again.

8 After five rounds, add your scores to find your final score. The player with the lower final score wins.

Variation

Write the score with plus and minus signs to show whether your total is less than or greater than 7,500. For example, if your total is 7,494, your score is –6. If your total is 7,502, your score is +2. Your goal is to get a final score for five rounds that is as close to 0 as possible.

SMH G3

◄ Games, G3

Index

J

Justification, 19, 125–127

L

Landmark numbers, 29–30, 98
LogoPaths **Software,** 13

M

Mathematical Emphases, 10–12, 15, 23, 55, 85
Mathematics in This Unit, 10–13
Math Focus Points, 10–12, 20, 23, 26, 32, 36, 43, 51, 55, 58, 64, 69, 75, 81, 85, 88, 93, 97, 105, 110
for Discussion, 52, 60, 65, 72, 82, 90, 95, 98, 106
Math Notes
"Above" and "Below" on the 10,000 Chart, 34
Algorithms, 77
Is the Number Line a Strategy?, 60
The U.S. Algorithm, 76
Using "Minus" Instead of "Take Away," 59
Using Positive Numbers Only, 76
Using the Equal Sign Correctly, 38
Math Workshop activities
Adding and Subtracting Large Numbers, 48–50, 52, 100–103, 108–109
Using Subtraction Strategies, 78–79, 84
Million, 11, 53
Missing parts problems, 16–17, 66–68
Money problems, 18
Multiples of 10, 100 and 1000
adding and subtracting large numbers with, 45–48, 52, 95, 137–139
in multiplication and division problems, 44–45
Multi-step problems, 11, 95, 100–101, 108

N

NCTM's Principles and Standards for School Mathematics, 128–130
Notation
for addition solutions, 38, 65–66, 98–103
for subtraction solutions, 65–66, 98–103, 119
Number line, 16, 17, 18–19, 37, 60, 73, 99, 106, 118, 120–121, 140–142, 145–146
Numbers. *See also* Place value.
counting to 10,000, 29
decomposition of, 10
landmarks, 29–30, 98
relationships, 10
writing and naming large numbers, 11, 52–54

O

Observing Students at Work. *See* Ongoing Assessment: Observing Students at Work.
Ongoing Assessment: Observing Students at Work, 14, 28, 31, 35, 38, 41–42, 49, 60, 62, 67, 72, 78, 89–90, 92, 95, 101, 111
Overview of This Unit, 8–9

P

Pictures, 74
Place value
adding and subtracting large numbers by, 45–48
adding multiples of 1,000, 27–28
base-ten number system and, 113–114
Closest Estimate. See Ten-Minute Math.
computational fluency and, 114–115
names of larger numbers, 10–11, 52–54
of numbers to 10,000, 28–31
of numbers to 100,000, 10, 33–35
Practicing Place Value. See Ten-Minute Math.
10,000 chart, 28–31, 113–114

Place-value strategy, 45–48, 70, 90, 95–96, 123, 141
Planners
Investigation Planners, 24–25, 56–57, 86–87
Today's Plan, 26, 32, 36, 43, 51, 58, 64, 69, 75, 81, 88, 93, 97, 105, 110
Portfolio opportunities, 14
Practice and Review in This Unit, 21
Practicing Place Value. See Ten-Minute Math.
Professional Development. *See* Dialogue Boxes; Teacher Notes.
Program components, 6–7
Proof, 126–127

R

Reasoning, 19, 73, 125–127
Related problems, 45–49, 52
Representation. *See also* Number line. 16–17, 18–19, 73

S

Starter problems, 70–72, 79, 84
Story contexts, 16–17, 18–19, 46–47, 73, 95, 103, 108
Student Math Handbook **minis,** 149–151
Subtracting back strategy, 16–17, 34, 59, 107, 119–120, 124, 140
Subtracting by place strategy, 12, 60, 76–79, 84, 122, 129
Subtracting down strategy. *See* Subtracting back strategy.
Subtracting in parts strategy, 59, 71, 119
Subtraction. *See also* Difference.
comparison problems, 16
distance problems, 66–68, 80, 84
missing parts problems, 16–17
of multiples of 100 and 1000, 11, 33–35, 37–40
notation for, 65–66, 118
place value and, 114–115
related problems, 45–48, 52
relationship to addition, 16–17, 37
starter problems, 70–72, 79, 84